Excel

BASIC SKILLS

ENGLISH

YEAR 5

AGES 10–11

ENGLISH WORKBOOK

PASCAL PRESS

Kristine Brown

Reprinted 2006, 2008, 2009, 2010 (twice), 2012, 2015, 2017, 2018, 2020, 2023

ISBN 978 1 74125 158 6

Pascal Press
PO Box 250
Glebe NSW 2037
(02) 9198 1748
www.pascalpress.com.au

Publisher: Vivienne Joannou
Project editor: Emma Driver
Edited by Christine Eslick
Page design and layout by Jelly Design
Typesetting by Alena Jencik, Grand Graphix Pty Ltd
Cover by DiZign Pty Ltd
Cover photos by Photos.com
Photo of Lion Gate (page 84) by Christine Eslick
Printed by Vivar Printing/Green Giant Press

Contents

Acknowledgements

I would like to thank the following students, authors and publishers for their very kind permission to use their writing in this book:

Tara Levy-Stephens, for her recount " Sport and Healthy Lifestyles Week" on page 2
James Colquhoun, for his recount on page 6
Jordan O' Rourke, for his newspaper report " Superior Springwood" on page 7
Andrew Little, for his story " Washed out" on page 10 (Andrew' s story was a Victorian regional winner in the 2004 Nestlé Write Around Australia Competition)
Scholastic Australia, for the writing tip by Paul Jennings on page 16 (from Eyespy Magazine, no. 5, 1993. Text copyright Scholastic Australia, 1993. First published by Scholastic Australia Pty Limited, 1993)
Elizabeth Honey and Allen & Unwin, for the poems " Squeezed fresh daily" and " Gel" and the illustrations (from *Mongrel Doggerel*) on page 18
Bill Condon, for the poems " Non-blister sister" and " Good old Ted" (from *Don't Throw Rocks at Chicken Pox*) on page 18
CSIRO Education, for the procedure " Make your own mini-hovercraft" (from *Scientriffic* magazine, No. 26, July/August 2003) on page 26
Adam Lucas, for his letter to author William Nicholson on page 34
William Nicholson, for his letter in reply to Adam Lucas on page 40
Hannah McLean, for her speech " Frogs" on page 42
Bradley Aldous, for his explanation " Venus Flytrap" on page 50
Erin Allen, for her explanation " The Pitcher of Death" on page 50

I would also like to thank Val Noake at the State Library of New South Wales and Nestlé Write Around Australia for their help and cooperation in relation to the use of Andrew Little' s story. Nestlé Write Around Australia is a Nestlé Good Life Program coordinated by the State Library of New South Wales and supported by state and public libraries around Australia.

My special thanks to the following teachers for advice and help with finding texts and for ideas on various aspects of the book:

Graeme Wilson, Julie Tomlins, Milly Kennedy, Jenny Williamson and Anne Wharton from Springwood Public School
Lyn Maloney from James Erskine Public School
Debbie Jay from Arndell Anglican College
Rhonda Bassett from Bowning Public School

Finally, my thanks go to the independent reviewers of the book for their thorough and constructive comments.

To the student

This book will help you with the writing you do every day at school—in English and in other subjects. Each chapter looks at a different type of writing. Some are imaginative types of texts such as narratives and poems. Others are factual types of texts such as reports and explanations.

All the chapters begin with a sample text. Make sure you read the sample text carefully and look at the special features marked on it.

You should then try the activities that follow. These give you guidance and practice in writing a similar type of text. Some activities help you with grammar and punctuation. Others focus on words—the way they are spelt and what they mean. Some activities are just for fun. Each chapter ends with activities that help you write a complete text yourself.

There are spaces in the workbook where you can write, but you will need your own paper for some of the writing activities at the end of most chapters. I suggest you buy a book or folder to put this writing in—let' s call it your **Writer's Notebook**. If you like, you could use your Writer' s Notebook for all the longer pieces of writing you do. It would also be a good place to put bits and pieces you collect as writing ideas—illustrations, advertisements, photographs, research information, and so on.

Always have a dictionary nearby as you work through the chapters. Be sure to ask for help if you need it.

It is best to work through the book from Chapter 1 to the end, because in this way you will build on skills from one chapter to the next. However, you could also use the chapters as you need them. For example, you could do Chapter 8, Writing a review, when you are doing this kind of writing at school.

Many of the sample texts throughout the book have been written by students of your own age. I really hope you enjoy reading them and then writing your own.

Have fun and good luck!

Kristine Brown

Chapter 1 Writing a personal recount

In a personal recount, your aim is to give details about events that you experienced. You tell what happened, in the order that it happened. You also make personal comments about events.

STRUCTURE

LANGUAGE

Sport and Healthy Lifestyles Week

Last week our school had a Sport and Healthy Lifestyles Week. The best day for me was Monday, because on Monday we had three activities—yoga, softball and cricket.

We first had yoga with Mrs Rowe and Mrs Godleman. We did all kinds of stretches and exercises. We also did the "salute to the sun". Mrs Godleman told us that in India they do the "salute to the sun" at dawn when the sun comes up. The children also do it at school in the morning. I liked yoga. It was very relaxing but it wasn't my favourite thing of the day.

After recess, we had softball with two instructors called Craig and Andrew. Before we started, the instructors explained the basic rules. Our team got to field first while the other team got to bat. I almost got a catch, but Josh pushed me out of the way and then he didn't even catch it himself! Then it came time for our team to bat. My first hit wasn't a very good hit and I got out. But my next two hits were really good (for me, anyway) and I got two home runs! I was extremely happy. I liked softball. It was my favourite activity of the day.

After lunch, we had cricket with an instructor called David. We were split into two groups. One group got to bowl at wickets while the other group got to hit balls at little cones. I got to bowl first with Ella, Sean and Jake. After bowling, I got to bat. I didn't like cricket as much as the other activities. I thought it was just a little bit boring, but the boys thought it was great.

On the other days we did tennis, taekwondo, athletics, tai chi, bocce, rugby league, gymnastics, aerobics and hockey. We really learned a lot about many different kinds of sport and we got pretty fit as well. Because I enjoyed softball so much, I have decided to do softball as my sport next year.

Tara Levy-Stephens

Orientation to topic: what, who, when, where

Series of events told in the order they occurred (chronological order)

Paragraphs organised by time periods

Personal comments on events

Conclusion includes a comment on events

Proper nouns to name individual people and places

Pronouns (e.g. *we*, *me*, *he*) instead of nouns

Interesting detail about events, people and places

Past tense verbs (e.g. *had*, *did*)

Time words and phrases to make order of events clear (e.g. *first*, *then*, *after*)

Thinking and feeling verbs to comment on events (e.g. *liked*, *thought*)

What did you read?

1. Why did Tara like Monday best? ____________________

2. Circle the best answer. The "salute to the sun" is:
   - a something that Tara does at school every morning.
   - b a special kind of yoga.
   - c something that people in India do at dawn.

3. Circle the best answer. Tara liked:
   - a yoga the most and cricket the least.
   - b softball the most and cricket the least.
   - c cricket the most and softball the least.

4. Why was Tara annoyed at Josh? (Give two reasons.) ____________________

   ____

5. What made Tara happy about her softball performance? ____________________

6. Who enjoyed the cricket? ____________________

How was it written?

1. The first paragraph of a recount should tell the reader who or what it is about, and where or when the events happened. What does the first paragraph here tell you about:

   what? ____________________ who? ____________________

   where? ____________________ when? ____________________

2. ***Then*** is a very overused word in recounts. In these sentences from the text, write down the words Tara uses instead of ***then*** to tell us the order in which things happened.

   - a ____________________, we had softball with two instructors called Craig and Andrew.
   - b ____________________, we had cricket with an instructor called David.
   - c ____________________, I got to bat.

3. Personal recounts are more interesting if you give some details, instead of just saying, "We did this, then we did that, then we did this, then we did that" and so on. What interesting detail does Tara give about yoga? ____________________

   ____

4. Personal recounts are about what has already happened, so the verbs are usually in the P ___ ___ ___ tense.

5. Circle the best answer. In a recount, it can be hard to cover everything that happened without making it boring. How does Tara manage to cover all the week's events without being boring?
   - a By saying just a little bit about each sport event of the week
   - b By giving detail about one day and then summarising the other days
   - c By skipping some activities altogether

6. Circle the best answer. Personal recounts usually end with some comments on the events experienced. What does Tara comment on?
   - a the whole week's activities
   - b only Monday's activities

Spelling and meaning

healthy	activities	exercises	favourite	thought
yoga	cricket	gymnastics	taekwondo	athletics
tai chi	bocce	rugby league	aerobics	hockey

Tip for special spellers

A good way to learn new spellings is the **look–say–cover–write–check** method:
Look hard at the word, especially the difficult parts.
Say it out loud. Close your eyes and picture it in your mind while you say it.
Cover it up.
Write it without looking back.
Check it.
If you get it right, write it once more. If you get it wrong, do the **look–say–cover–write–check** method again till you get it right.

1 Try out the **look–say–cover–write–check** method on the first line of words in the word box. Use the lines below.

____________	____________	____________
____________	____________	____________
____________	____________	____________
____________	____________	____________
____________	____________	____________

Did it work for you? (Yes? No? Sometimes?) ____________________

2 Words ending in a consonant + ***y*** make plurals by changing the ***y*** to ***i*** and then adding ***es*** (e.g. activity → activit***ies***). Can you make the plurals of these words?

try ____________ pony ____________ party ____________

library ____________ territory ____________ boundary ____________

3 Choose one of the words from the word box to describe each picture.

a

b

c

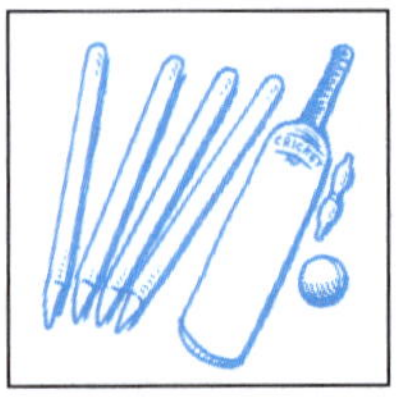

d

e

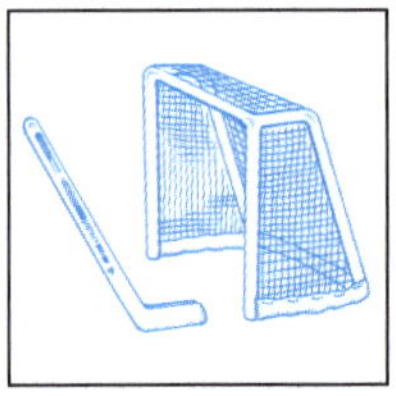

f

a ___________

b ___________

c ___________

d ___________

e ___________

f ___________

4 The English language has borrowed many words from other languages. Four words from the word box are from other languages. Can you guess the answers to these questions?

a Which word is from Korean and means "foot, hand, way"? ______________

b Which word is from Italian and means "balls"? ______________

c Which word is from Chinese and means "fist of the Great Absolute"? ______________

d Which word is from Hindi and means "union"? ______________

e Do you know any other foreign words we use in sports? ______________

Grammar—Nouns and pronouns

You probably know that **nouns** are words that name people, places, things and ideas in our world. Examples of nouns from the text are ***school***, ***exercises***, ***gymnastics***, ***thing***, ***Monday***, ***Mrs Rowe*** and ***India***.

Two important kinds of nouns are:

- **common nouns**, which name people, places and things in a **general** way (e.g. ***school***, ***exercises***, ***gymnastics***)
- **proper nouns**, which name **particular** people, places and things (e.g. ***Monday***, ***Mrs Rowe***, ***India***).

We can sometimes use **pronouns** to take the place of nouns in a text. One important kind of pronoun is the personal pronoun: ***I***, ***you***, ***he***, ***she***, ***it***, ***we***, ***they***, ***me***, ***him***, ***her***, ***us*** and ***them***.

When we use a pronoun it should be **absolutely clear** which noun it refers to. If it is not clear, we need to use a noun instead.

1 Can you find all the nouns and personal pronouns in this paragraph from a recount? Underline the common nouns, double underline the proper nouns and (circle) the pronouns. The first ones have been done for you.

On Wednesday, (we) walked to the Birraway Art Gallery, about two kilometres away. We looked at the paintings and sculptures. Some of the sculptures were absolutely huge. Afterwards, we had a lesson in cartooning with a cartoonist called Nick. He taught us some cool tricks to do when drawing figures, for example, how to show a person is moving. My cartoon was not the best (Kyle's and Tanama's were best as usual), but it was much better than the cartoons I usually do.

2 In the sentences below, it is not absolutely clear what the circled pronouns refer to. Can you substitute a noun instead? (You might have to use more than one word, and sometimes there might be two possible answers.)

a When the boys did the dance in front of the girls, (they) all cheered. ______________

b The drama activities in our Creative Arts Week were my favourite. (She) taught us a Chinese Whispers game using actions instead of words. ______________

c On Wednesday we had a henna art class in the hall. (It) is a kind of tattoo. ______________

d I made my billy-cart out of an old bike, and Joe made his out of a lawnmower. (It) went really well. ______________

e The drama teacher asked Lina and Josie to help her with an activity. First, she gave (her) a piece of blank paper. ______________

Punctuation—Commas to separate items in a list

We use **commas** for many different reasons. In these sentences, the commas **separate items in a list**.

Examples On Monday we had three activities—yoga**,** softball and cricket.
I got to bowl first with Ella, Sean and Jake.
On the other days we did tennis, taekwondo, athletics, tai chi, bocce, rugby league, gymnastics, aerobics and hockey.

Did you notice that we don't use a comma between the second last and last item in each list? We write "and" instead.

Can you put the commas in the right places in these sentences?

a Jenna does gymnastics and likes the parallel bars the vault and the mat the best.
b Marko does three winter sports—soccer ice hockey and gymnastics.
c Our teacher told us to bring sports shoes a hat sunscreen a jacket and lunch money.
d We do exercises before school on Monday Tuesday Wednesday and Friday.
e In our last three matches we won drew and lost.
f Forehands backhands and volleys are all types of tennis strokes.

Can you help?

James wrote this recount of the Sport and Healthy Lifestyles Week. His recount is interesting because he has made comments about the events. However, we have taken some of them out and put them in the box. Can you put them back where they belong?

That was definitely the highlight of the week. The helmets were the best. It could put you to sleep! Tai chi was borrring! (YES!) In conclusion it was the best school week ever! I got 5.5.

In Sport and Healthy Lifestyles Week, the first thing we did was yoga with Mrs Rowe and Mrs Godleman.

_______________ Then we did softball with Craig and Andrew.

_______________ Then we played cricket with David Stanford. It was so much fun! The next day we did netball and tai chi. _______________.

Wednesday was the teachers' strike _______ so nobody went to school. On Thursday we did the obstacle course. _______________

After the break we did the beep test.* _______________ Afterwards we did rugby league. The next day we had to get to school early so we could walk to tennis. It was really good fun.

Later we did Coach Approach—there were five activities and handball was the best. _______________

____

James Colquhoun

* The Beep Test is a fitness test where you have to run at ever-increasing speed between two points. The pace is set by a machine that makes a 'beep' noise. Each person gets a score.

Puzzle time

1 All these words are to do with sport, but they are missing their first and last letters. Can you work them out? (The picture gives you a clue about some of the words.)

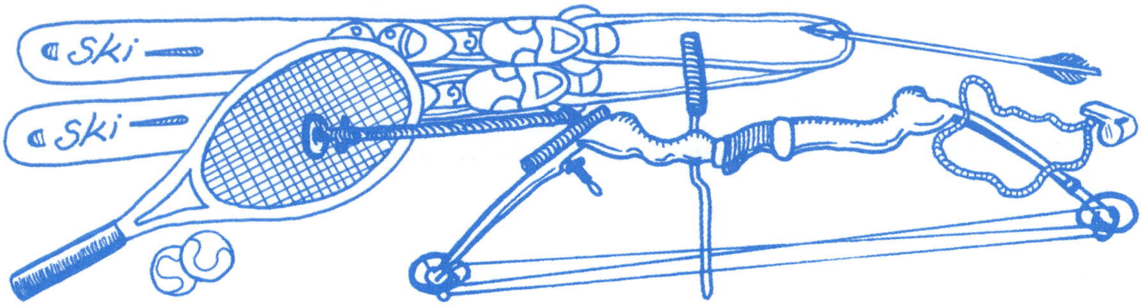

___ RCHER ___	___ ATC ___	___ OUR ___
___ KIIN ___	___ IVIN ___	___ ACHTIN ___
___ OALPOS ___	___ HOTPU ___	___ APTAI ___
___ EFERE ___	___ ACQUE ___	___ MPIR ___

2 Can you unscramble these letters? The answer is what you will be if you play lots of sport.

EYHLATH ______________________

Your turn to write

Tips for incredibly interesting writers

When writing personal recounts, make your writing really interesting by:

- focusing on the most interesting or important events;
- leaving out boring or unimportant events;
- giving details about particular people and events;
- making comments about events.

1 This student's recount, written as a newspaper report, follows all the tips above about writing an interesting recount. Read the recount and then answer the short questions on page 8.

Superior Springwood

By reporter Jordan O'Rourke

SPS travelled to Lawson Pool yesterday and all competitive swimmers did wonderfully.

As the day went on, the house points went up and up and all the spectators were amazed by the rocket arms and legs as the swimmers got pumped.

In the boys' 100 metre freestyle one student kept on swimming after a false start, not hearing the teachers yelling "Stop!" from the side of the pool. Luckily Samuel Walton caught the swimmer and stopped him as he got out of the pool.

When asked about his feelings on catching the competitor, Samuel stated, "I felt good but I was a bit puffed out after catching him."

All the non-swimmers were waiting for free time as Adam snapped Andrew's nose and blood went everywhere. Mr Gillis was kept busy hosing the blood away.

Finally, after the day was over, SPS students returned to school for the awards ceremony which was held in the library.

After the relieved swimming champions were photographed, the swimmers went home tired but proud.

a Does Jordan recount the events in order? (Yes/No) ______________________

b Does he give detail of every swimming event? (Yes/No) ______________________

c Which event of the day does he give most space to, and why? ______________________

____

____

2 Now write a paragraph about **one event** only to add to Jordan's recount. Use your own experiences of swimming carnivals and your imagination. Here are a few ideas.

- A surprise win by a student
- The most exciting race of the day
- A race where one student swims an extra length
- The teachers' race

____

____

____

____

____

____

____

____

____

____

____

3 The pictures below show what happened to one class on an excursion to the museum. Use the pictures and your imagination to write a recount of the events.

- Begin by giving information about who, what, when, where.
- Write the events in the order that they happened.
- Focus on the most interesting events.
- Try to use other time words instead of ***then***.
- Add details about what happened.
- Give some personal comments.
- Add a conclusion to round off your recount and make an overall comment on the day.
- Proofread your writing for correct spelling, punctuation and grammar.

Orientation

Events

Conclusion

Chapter 2 Writing a narrative

In a narrative, your aim is to tell a story about events in a way that interests and entertains the reader.

STRUCTURE

LANGUAGE

Washed out

This was supposed to be an exciting adventure!

My brother and I were sitting in an old canoe at dawn on the first morning of our holiday. We were exploring unknown territory. It felt as if I was king of the world! No one else would be awake for hours. The lake around us was still and shrouded in mist. Water birds were starting to stir. An invisible frog was croaking in a nearby clump of rushes.

As usual the only snag was my brother. Once again he started being a total pain. He kept complaining about how cold and wet his feet were, and because he wouldn't sit still the canoe was rocking and taking in splashes of freezing water.

"You're so useless. Can't you even row in the right direction?"

"Of course I can but you can't steer, you jerk."

"Why are you trying to rock us overboard?"

"Because I'm trying not to be hit by your oar, you clumsy oaf!"

As we argued, the boat kept changing direction. Suddenly there was an enormous thump and we were both knocked backwards off our seats.

The boat had hit a log and we were taking in water. That was when we realised that the mist had thickened and our surroundings were totally invisible. We were all by ourselves, surrounded by dense cloud. We didn't have a clue where dry land was. We were lost like helpless little children in a big city. It was really scary!

I started paddling frantically forwards and Alex started paddling backwards. The canoe was spinning in circles. I felt sick and dizzy. The water had reached our ankles and was rising. "What are we going to do?" wailed Alex. "We're going ... we're going to die!"

I'd never seen my brother totally scared before. The only way we might get out of this would be another first—working together.

Frantically I screamed to Alex to take off his shoe and start bailing. I grabbed the oars and started rowing as fast as I could towards the bird sounds we could hear in the shallow water. This was no way to learn how to row!

We were both exhausted. The boat started to sink from under us. We started screaming for help as the water swooshed up our chests.

Then, unbelievably, the sun came out and the mist disappeared.

We found ourselves knee deep in freezing water, two metres from a row of curious family members eating breakfast.

I have never been so embarrassed in my entire life. I think my brother must have felt the same.

The release from absolute panic was just too much. We looked at each other's mud-smeared faces and started roaring with laughter.

Although our 'great' adventure had turned out to be a complete washout, my brother and I, for that moment anyway, had been friends!

Andrew Little

Structure annotations:

Orientation: who, what, where and when

Short paragraphs to help build interest and tension

Complication: an unusual or interesting event or series of events

Climax: the highest point of excitement or tension in the story

Resolution: the complication is 'resolved' in some way (the problem is solved or an answer is found)

Comment (or coda) on events (e.g. a lesson to be learnt)

Language annotations:

Opening sentence instantly gets reader's attention

Descriptive language

First person narration (*I, we*) but many stories are narrated in third person (*he, she*)

Dialogue to make story lively

Action verbs

Saying verbs

Thinking/ feeling verbs

Past tense

Adverbs and adverbial phrases to talk about how, why, where and when

What did you read?

1 True or false?

a The adventure happened when the boys were on holiday. ______

b There was no mist before the boys started their adventure. ______

c The boys' only problem was hitting a log. ______

d Alex realised they had to work together to save themselves. ______

2 Circle the best answer. The boys were embarrassed because:

a they were panicking when the water was really very shallow.

b the family nearby saw them panicking.

c both a and b.

3 Story writers don't always give you every detail about events. You have to work these out from other information given. Answer these questions using the information given in the text. Give your reasons.

a Do you think the boys' parents knew they were out on the water? ______

______

b Do you think Alex is the younger or older brother? ______

______

c Do you think the boys will still fight after their adventure? ______

______

4 Andrew's story is about *more* than a boating incident.

a What else is it about? ______

b Can you think of a different title for the story to describe this other theme?

______

How was it written?

1 Andrew gives us clues in the orientation that something will go wrong.

a What are the **first** words that do this? ______

b Which words tell us what or who will probably make it go wrong? ______

______

2 Andrew uses dialogue to add interest to the story. Tick the best answer.
Andrew uses the first dialogue to show:

a how annoying his brother is.

b how he and Alex relate to one another.

c how hard it is to row a small boat.

(*Hint*: He does not say who said what.)

3 The narrator's feelings change many times after feeling "king of the world". Can you underline all the words and phrases that describe his feelings during the adventure?

4 Andrew uses some very expressive words to describe what happens. Which word does he use instead of the following more common ones?

a covered (para. 2) ______________________ b wake up (para. 2) ______________________

c problem (para. 3) ______________________ d stupid person (para. 4) ______________________

5 Circle the best answer. A concluding comment can help us understand a narrative. This one shows that the narrator:

a appreciates the experience he shared with his brother.
b will never do something like this with his brother again.
c will be more careful when he goes out in a boat again.

Spelling and meaning

canoe	unknown	invisible	steer	clumsy
backwards	realised	surroundings	totally	forwards
exhausted	disappeared	curious	breakfast	embarrassed

Tip for super spellers

A good trick for learning words with unusual spellings is to invent a **spelling pronunciation**. That means you **say** the words in a way that reminds you of their spelling. For example, say these words out loud the way they are written here:

can–OH–EE un–K–nown invis–EYE–ble BREAK–fast ex–HOR–sted

1 Which word from the word box am I thinking of?

a How you might feel at the end of a long run ______________________

b Impossible to be seen ______________________

c You do this with cars, bikes and boats ______________________

d The opposite of 'appeared' ______________________

e Everything around you ______________________

f You might go red in the face if you feel like this ______________________

g You might not get a job as a waiter if you are like this ______________________

h Completely, absolutely ______________________

i Understood ______________________

Andrew uses some good sound words in his story, for example:

- ***swoosh*** to describe the water rushing over them as the boat sank
- ***croak*** to describe the noise the frogs made
- ***roar*** to describe their laughter
- ***thump*** to describe the boat hitting the log.

2 Choose one of the sound words from the box on page 13 to use in the sentences that follow. Add ***-ed*** or ***-ing*** if you need to. (There is more than one possible answer.)

Example I could hear nothing but the __rustle__ of the leaves.

rustle	buzz	whisper	hum	crash	gurgle	boom
rumble	rattle	trill	chirrup	thud	whistle	chatter

a The ______________________ of the cicadas was deafening.

b The thunder ______________________ in the distance.

c The wind ______________________ through the forest.

d The creek ______________________ down the mountainside.

e I could hear the happy ______________________ of the birds.

f The trucks ______________________ along the bumpy track.

g The trees fell to the ground with a ______________________.

Grammar—Simple sentences

Let's revise what you know about simple sentences.
A simple sentence has only one meaningful message (a **clause**). It has a **subject** and a **verb**.
Look at these sentences (the subjects are in **bold** and the verbs are underlined):

Examples **We** <u>were exploring</u> unknown territory.
I <u>felt</u> sick and dizzy.
The canoe <u>was spinning</u> in circles.
It <u>was</u> really scary.
As usual **the only snag** <u>was</u> my brother.

The **subject** is what the sentence is about. It usually includes a noun (e.g. ***canoe***, ***snag***) or a pronoun (e.g. ***we***, ***I***, ***it***). Sometimes there are other words before the subject (e.g. ***as usual***).
The **verb** is the word that tells us what someone or something is doing, saying, thinking, feeling, being or having (e.g. ***were exploring***, ***felt***, ***was spinning***, ***was***).

1 In these sentences from the story, circle the subjects and underline the verbs. (*Hint:* To find the subject, ask yourself **who** or **what** the sentence is about.)

a My brother and I were sitting in an old canoe at dawn on the first morning of our holiday.
b No one else would be awake for hours.
c The lake around us was still and shrouded in mist.
d Water birds were starting to stir.
e An invisible frog was croaking in a nearby clump of rushes.
f Once again he started being a total pain.
g We were lost like helpless little children in a big city.

2 Can you unscramble these simple sentences? (*Hint:* Find the verb first and then work out a possible subject.)

a afterwards turned Mr Shortly Stanovski corner the. ______________________________

____

b lined the small up at Ten counter boys. ______________________________

____

c simply I could the steer bike not. ______________________

____

d stayed silent Sanjay completely. ______________________

____

e us laughed from The the at kookaburra treetops. ______________________

____

Punctuation—Quotation marks and punctuating dialogue

You need to use quotation (or speech) marks to show exactly what people said.
Example "What are we going to do?" wailed Alex. "We're going … we're going to die!"
You can use **single ('…') or double ("…") quotation marks** for dialogue but, whichever you use, stick to the same method throughout your text. Your teacher will tell you which method to use.
The best way to work out where to put capital letters, full stops, question marks and exclamation marks when writing dialogue is to look at examples:
Examples Marty said "He told Josh everything." OR "He told Josh everything," Marty said.
He cried "Help me, help me!" OR "Help me, help me!" he cried.
She asked "How do you know that?" OR "How do you know that?" she asked.
"Fishing," she said, "is a stupid waste of time." OR "Fishing is a stupid waste of time," she said.

Extra! We can use single quotation marks to show we are using a word in a special way. In the last paragraph Andrew writes: *Although our 'great' adventure had turned out to be a complete washout* … He is saying that their adventure was, in fact, the opposite of 'great'.

Can you put quotation marks and other punctuation where needed in these sentences?

a Let me go she screamed
b Why can't I come with you now she asked
c Sit still he shouted or the boat will go over
d I will show them I whispered to myself
e I don't know where he is now she cried softly
f You'll be very sorry she said because I won't forget this quickly
g Then I heard her say come over here I'm under the dinner table
h Josie asked when will I be able to go home

JOKE
Do you know these famous authors?
Exploring the Pole by Ann Tarctic
The Tiger's Revenge by Claude Leg
Be Prepared by Justin Case
Keeping Pet Snakes by Sir Pent
The Speed Trap by Ray Dar

Can you help?

You often begin a narrative by describing a scene. This student wants to put this picture into words to begin a story about an unusual adventure at the beach. Can you help?

It was an ordinary morning at Emerald Beach.

Puzzle time

Andrew writes that Alex ***wailed***. He does not write that Alex ***said***. There are many good words to use instead of ***say*** or ***said*** in your narratives. The ones below have their first and second syllables muddled up (e.g. PRO/PER and WHIS/TEST give PROTEST AND WHISPER). Can you match the correct syllables and write them below?

STAM/TER	SPUT/MER	MUMB/TER	CHAT/MENT
COM/LAIN	SNIFF/MISE	PRO/MUR	AN/CLARE
MUT/LE	COMP/NOUNCE	DE/TER	MUR/LE

Your turn to write

Tip for totally terrific writers

Check out this terrific tip from a great story writer, Paul Jennings:

"I think kids should really value their own life experiences … A little embarrassing experience you've had, or your dog dying, can be very real and very moving if you can weave it into your stories. If everything is magical, people don't relate to it. If you make the reader feel that it is the real world, then, when something fantastic happens, it has an enormous amount of power."

1 As Paul Jennings says, your everyday experiences are a good place to start when writing a narrative. One way to make an everyday experience into a narrative is to ask the question "What if?"

Think about an everyday walk home from school with your best friend. Imagine what might happen IF you found a lost dog … or a small child … or a million dollars. Or, imagine IF you met a very, very old man ... or … someone who looked very much like Harry Potter ... or … an alien!
All these ideas could make an ordinary experience into a story worth telling. Let's try it out. Next to each everyday situation below, write at least one "what if" event like those above.

a *What if* while on the school bus ____________________

b *What if* while at the rubbish tip ____________________

c *What if* when running a race ____________________

d *What if* while staying with a grandparent ____________________

e *What if* while driving with mum or dad ____________________

2 Now choose one of your ideas as the starting point for a narrative (or use an idea about Emerald Beach from page 15). First, jot down a few ideas in the space below. Think about these questions.

- How will I set up the story (the orientation)?
- How will I get the reader's attention at the start?
- How will I introduce the complication—the "what if" part?
- How will I resolve the story (resolution)? Will it be funny? happy? sad? serious? magical?
- Will I add a comment (coda) on the events?

3 a Now write a draft of your story on the following lines. Use dialogue and interesting words to make your story come alive. Check your spelling, punctuation and grammar.

Orientation (Who? What? When? Where?) ____________________

____

____

Complication (What happens that is unusual, interesting, funny, sad or 'out of this world'?)

Resolution (How does everything work out? Does it work out well? badly? funnily?)

Coda (What would you like to say about the story or characters? Is there a lesson to be learnt?)

b Now write your story out again on your own paper or in your Writer's Notebook (see page 1).

Chapter 3 Writing a poem

Poems aim to express ideas and feelings about human experiences. Poems are usually meant to be read out loud, so the sound of the language is important. (Be sure to read these poems out loud before doing the activities.)

STRUCTURE

Interesting titles

Poems come in ***many shapes and forms***. The first three poems have a regular rhythm (beat) and line length, but the last poem does not.

Rhyme (e.g. *doors, Jaws; miss you, kiss you; nibbled on, dribbled on* (not all poems use rhyme)

Final lines usually round off ideas (e.g. make a joke)

LANGUAGE

Words create ***clear images*** (e.g. *lurk* to describe what mothers do)

Comparing one thing to another (***similes***)

Alliteration (repetition of consonant sounds)

Short phrases for rhythm and interest

Freedom with language—words and grammar used in unusual ways

Squeezed fresh daily

Mothers lurk behind doors
And lunge at you like Jaws
Making careers out of things in your ears
Saying how much they miss you
Finding excuses to kiss you.

Elizabeth Honey

Non-blister sister

Exams are such an awful pain
They give me blisters on the brain.
I wish I was my sister Ruth—
She's so smart,
She's blister-proof.

Bill Condon

Gel

People notice you're about
if all your hair is sticking out.
Gel will make your hair look slick.
(Another thing—it's very quick!)
Feeling flat?
Soon fix that!
What the hell!
Slap on the gel!

Elizabeth Honey

Good old Ted

Eye gouges,
Ear tugs,
Bumps,
Thumps and
Falls.
Dribbled on,
Nibbled on,
Bounced off the walls.
Cuddled so often he's lost all his hair.
Just how much
Can a teddy bear
Bear?

Bill Condon

Poems and drawings by Elizabeth Honey from *Mongrel Doggerel*, Allen & Unwin, 1998. Poems by Bill Condon from *Don't Throw Rocks at Chicken Pox*, Angus&Robertson, 1993. Poems and drawings printed with permission.

What did you read?

1. a Look at the title of the first poem. What do we usually think of that is ***squeezed fresh daily***?

   ____

   b Who or what is being squeezed fresh daily in the poem? ______________________

2. Circle the best answer. In the first poem, what does ***Making careers out of things in your ears*** mean?
   a Mothers spend a lot of their time looking at their children's ears.
   b Mothers' jobs include looking at their children's ears.
   c Mothers can't have careers because they have to take care of their children.

3. Circle the best answer. In the third poem, what does ***People notice you're about*** mean?
   a People give you more attention.
   b People think you are stupid.
   c People see what kind of person you are.

4. Circle the best answer. The last poem is about how the teddy bear:
   a is very old and ugly.
   b is unloved.
   c is loved but not well taken care of.

5. In the last poem, what does the word ***gouges*** mean? (*Hint:* Think about what might happen to an old teddy's eyes.)

   ____

6. In the last poem, what does the second ***bear*** mean in ***Just how much / Can a teddy bear / Bear?***

   ____

How were they written?

1. The first poem uses interesting verbs to express how people move. Write the verb used instead of:

   a hide ______________ b move forwards ______________

2. Which very vivid image is used in the second poem to describe the effect of exams?

   ____

3. Poets often use phrases (groups of words) instead of sentences to 'sharpen' the picture of a thing or experience. Write the short phrase used instead of these sentences in the last poem.

   a Ted has gouges out of his eyes. ______________________

   b Ted has had many bumps, thumps and falls. ______________________

   c Ted has been nibbled on. ______________________

4. Poets also use phrases to keep the rhythm regular and fast. Write the words the poet left out before these words in the third poem to help the rhythm.

   a __________ __________ feeling flat? b __________ __________ soon fix that!

5. Why does the poet use short, fast lines in the last half of "Gel"? (*Hint:* Think about hair gel.)

   ____

   ____

6 All the poems are about subjects most children are familiar with. Which poem did you like most and why? ______________________________

____

Spelling and meaning

squeezed	daily	lurk	lunge	career
excuses	people	notice	slick	gel
blister	gouges	dribbled	bounced	cuddled

Tip for super smart spellers

Always put ***ge*** for the sound ***j*** at the end of a word (e.g. lun***ge***, gou***ge***). We never end a word with the letter ***j***. This "soft ***g***" also occurs before ***e***, ***i*** and ***y*** (e.g. ***g***el, en***g***ine, biolo***gy***, ur***g***ent).

1 Can you unscramble these words from the word box?

a aildy ____________
b iceton ____________
c dldduec ____________
d rreeac ____________
e lebdibrd ____________
f ggseou ____________
g klsci ____________
h usseexc ____________
i ppeeol ____________
j ouencdb ____________

2 Words that rhyme might not be spelt the same way. Can you think of words that rhyme with these words from the word box, using the clues given? (Some are not spelt the same way.)

squeeze	**gel**	**excuse (noun)**	**dribble**
____________ (a wind)	____________ (shout)	____________ (large bird)	____________ (eat a little)
____________ (bless you!)	____________ (ring a ding)	____________ (large mammal)	____________ (small argument)
____________ (make happy)	____________ (say)	____________ (man's name)	____________ (write quickly)

3 ***Lurk*** describes how a person waits in hiding or in secret—usually with an evil intention—for something to happen. People might lurk in shadows, lurk in dark alleyways, lurk in corridors, lurk outside closed doors or lurk in bushes. Other words to describe how a person might wait are ***linger***, ***loiter***, ***prowl***, ***cool their heels***, ***wait in ambush***. Use your dictionary to look up their meanings, and then match them to the descriptions below.

a One street gang waiting in hiding for a rival gang to turn into their street ____________

b An animal waiting for his prey to emerge from a cave ____________ c Trouble-makers waiting near the school gates ______

d People waiting outside a stage door, hoping to see the stars of the show ______

e A person waiting for a bus that comes every hour, after just missing one ______

Grammar—Phrases and similes

A **phrase** is a group of words that does not contain a complete verb.
Some phrases contain a part of a verb:
Example Squeezed fresh daily
Squeezed is part of a verb but it needs a helper word—***am***, ***is***, ***are***—to make it complete.

Other phrases contain adjectives and nouns:
Examples Good old Ted With red hair Smooth as silk
Phrases can be more effective than complete sentences in lines of poetry. They can help with rhythm, and at the same time they can "sharpen" the images for the audience.
Examples ***Finding excuses to kiss you*** instead of ***Mothers always try to find excuses to kiss you.***
Eye gouges instead of ***Ted has gouges out of his eyes.***

1 Can you change these sentences into short phrases that might be suitable in a poem? Leave out words like ***is***, ***are***, ***my***, ***we***, ***here***. You might want to change the word order or the form of the words.
Example My dog is a scruffy old dog. → Scruffy old dog

a We went over the bridge and past the cave. ______

b They are tiring, lazy days. ______

c The teacher glares at me. ______

d I spin around fast on my skates. ______

e There are children squealing. ______

f The rooms are dark and cold. ______

g We wear woolly socks and long underwear. ______

Similes are figures of speech in which one thing is said to be or behave **like** another.
Example Mothers … lunge at you like Jaws. (like the huge shark in the film *Jaws*)

We also make similes using the construction **as … as**.
Examples As black as a moonless night.
As awful as my mother's favourite perfume

2 Look at these students' similes. Can you write a different simile for the same adjectives?

a As skinny as a sausage ______

b As funny as Mr Bean ______

c As strong as a turnip ______

d As light as a helium balloon ______________________________

e As angry as a volcano ______________________________

f As tall as Mt Everest ______________________________

g As silly as a puppy ______________________________

h As polite as the Queen ______________________________

i As boring as my mum's opera music ______________________________

Punctuation—Punctuating poems

In poetry, we have **more freedom with punctuation** than in other writing. Sometimes we use punctuation in the usual way to break up ideas and make our meaning clear. However, we can also use it to actually suggest the ideas, images or feelings we are writing about.

1 Go back to "Squeezed fresh daily" and look at the punctuation. Read the poem out loud.

a Did the lack of punctuation make you read the poem at fast, slow or normal speed?

____

b Did it make you read it in a smooth, flowing way or a snappy, stop-start way?

____

c The punctuation suggests the way mothers move quickly and smoothly to catch their children and clean their ears. Read the poem again now with this image in mind.

2 Go back to "Gel" and look at the punctuation. Read the poem out loud.

a Did the frequent use of full stops and exclamation marks make you read the poem at fast, slow or normal speed? ______________________________

b How did it affect the rhythm? Was it smooth and flowing, or snappy?

____

c The punctuation reflects the fast, slick, snappy way we put hair gel on. Read the poem again now with this image in mind.

Can you help?

In "Non-blister sister" the poet writes ***blisters on the brain*** to create a vivid image of the way his head feels when he does a test or an exam. The image tells us exactly how painful he finds the experience, because we all know how terrible skin blisters feel.

Can you help this student write a poem about his old aunt coming to visit? The student has written most of the poem but can't decide on the best images to describe what she is like. He has jotted down some ideas in the box on the next page. Which images would you choose to fill in the blank spaces? You can add to or change the words as needed. You could express the image as a simile if you want (using ***like*** or ***as … as***).

Old Aunt Jess
Arrives tonight
Where can we hide from
her big wet kisses

______________________________ (What does the kiss feel like?)

her terrible perfume

______________________________. (What does her perfume smell like?)

How can we stand
listening to her stories

______________________________ (What is it like to listen to her stories?)

hearing her music

______________________________ (What does her music sound like?)

Eating her favourite foods
Mmmm. Chocolate.
Ding dong!
Hi! Come in!
Dear Aunt Jess.

Being trapped in a spider web	Being sucked up by a vacuum cleaner
Being held under water	Smoke alarms going off
Fingernails across the blackboard	Being trapped in jungle vines
Walking through wet sand	Squawking of cockatoos
The compost heap	Old socks or shoes
Being dumped by a big wave	Rotten eggs
Toffee burning	Watching the clothes dryer go round

Puzzle time

There are three traditional poems muddled up here. Can you sort the lines out? (Write them out on your own paper.)

Through the teeth
I met a man who wasn't there
Shooting submarines
Order in the court
Here it comes!
And past the gums
He wasn't there again today
His wife is in the bathtub
As I was going up the stair
Oh, how I wish he'd go away.
The judge is eating beans
Look out stomach

DID YOU KNOW?
The shortest poem in the world is called "Fleas".
It goes like this:
Adam
Had 'em.

Your turn to write

Tips for powerful poets

It is a good idea to read your poem out loud as you are writing it to see how it sounds. You'll find out which words work and which words don't.

And remember, poems don't have to rhyme. Rhyming can help to give a poem rhythm and beat, but it can also make you write thoughts and ideas that just don't make sense.

Read lots of poetry. Ask your school or local librarian to help you find poets—like Elizabeth Honey or Bill Condon—who write specially for children.

The poems on page 18 were about everyday things—people in our lives (mothers, sisters) and things we own or use (teddy bears, hair gel). The two poets wrote about these topics in a way that made us think about them in a new or interesting way.

1 Now try doing the same with people in *your* life. Follow the steps below to write a poem.

a Choose your topic. Here are some suggestions.

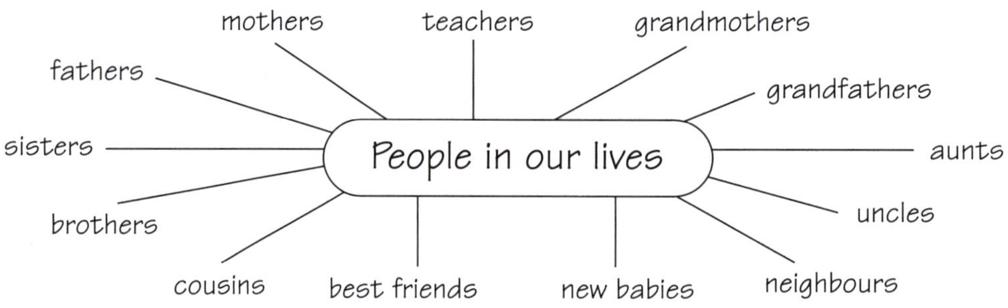

b Now think long and hard about your topic. Close your eyes and imagine being with the people you are writing about. Use the questions below to jot down some ideas.

What do these people look like? Sound like? Smell like? Move like?
What do they do for you?
What do you do when you are with them?
Where do you usually spend time with them?
What kinds of things do they say?
What do you love about them?
What is funny about them?
What annoys you?

c Draft your poem on the lines below.

- Use words and images to help your reader understand your ideas.
- Use phrases instead of full sentences if they help the rhythm and sharpen the images.

- Use rhyme only if it helps to express an idea.
- Use punctuation to help you suggest ideas and feelings.
- Read your poem out loud a few times as you write and see how it sounds.
- Revise it if needed till you are happy with it, and check your spelling.

d Write your poem out neatly and draw a picture to go with it. You could write it in your Writer's Notebook, or put it up where people will see it.

2 Are you ready for one more poem? Let's try a poem about a special thing you own or use. Follow the same three steps. Use your own paper or your Writer's Notebook.

- Here are some ideas for topics.

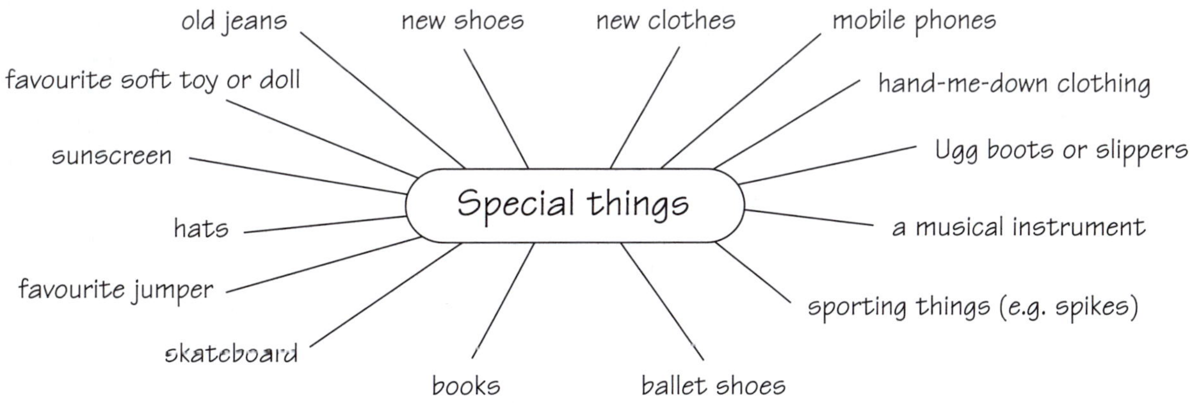

- Here are some questions to prompt your thinking.

What do you do with these things? How do they feel? smell? look? sound?
How do they make you feel? How do they make you look? Why do you love or hate them?

Chapter 4 Writing a procedure

In a procedure, your aim is to tell your reader exactly how to do or make something.

Make your own mini-hovercraft

Hovercrafts hover above the ground on a cushion of air. They can glide over land, ice or even water—they literally float on air! You can make your own mini-hovercraft with a few simple things from home.

You will need

- An old or unwanted CD (Ask someone BEFORE you use it!)
- An empty plastic reel of thread with a hole through the middle (NOT a reel with thin cardboard centre)
- Strong craft glue
- A big balloon

What to do

1. Glue the reel on top of the CD, so that the hole in the reel lines up exactly with the hole in the CD.
2. Wait a couple of hours for the glue to dry.
3. When the glue is dry, blow up your balloon and twist the end to stop the air from escaping.
4. Carefully stretch the neck of the balloon over the top of the reel. Make sure it is firmly attached.
5. Put the hovercraft on a flat, smooth surface. A kitchen benchtop is a good spot because it usually has no bumps.
6. Let go of the balloon quickly. Your hovercraft should start moving. If it doesn't, try giving it a couple of gentle pushes.

You're off!

So how does it work?
The air in the balloon goes under the CD very quickly and this pushes up the CD and allows it to move over the surface. And this is just how a real hovercraft works! A huge fan on top of the hovercraft pumps air underneath very quickly. As more and more air is trapped, the hovercraft is pushed up, and this allows it to move.

Adapted with permission from *Scientriffic*, No. 26, July/August 2003

STRUCTURE

- ***Goal or aim*** of the instructions
- ***Headings***
- ***Items you will need*** (not always included)
- ***Numbered steps*** for the reader to follow
- ***Helpful tips***
- ***End comment***
- ***Picture*** to help the reader
- Sometimes ***extra information*** explaining why things happen

LANGUAGE

- ***Punctuation and highlighting*** to draw attention to important information
- ***Common nouns***
- ***Command form of verbs*** (imperative), usually at start of a step
- ***Action verbs***
- ***Precise language***
- ***Adverbs*** to tell *how* to do actions
- ***When and if clauses***
- ***Short clear sentences***

What did you read?

1 Hovercrafts float on ______________________________.

2 True or false?

a You can use any type of cotton reel to make the hovercraft. __________

b You put the reel through the middle of the CD. __________

c You don't tie the end of the balloon. __________

d You hold the hovercraft tightly as it moves. __________

3 In which order do you do these steps? (Write number 1, 2 or 3.)

Blow up a balloon. ______ Use glue. ______ Stretch the balloon neck. ______

4 Fill in the blanks. The balloon hovercraft works because the __________ from the __________ forms a cushion between the __________ and the __________.

How was it written?

1 The procedure is structured to help the reader know what to do. If you wanted to do this experiment, what would be the first part you would read closely? (Give a reason.)

____

____

____

2 The command verbs (imperative form) are mostly at the start of the sentences in the "What to do" section, but not always. Underline all the verb commands in steps 1–6. (*Hint:* There are nine and some are not just single words.)

3 Circle the best answer. The command verbs are at the start of sentences because:

a they make it easier for the reader to follow the instructions.

b it is easier to write sentences that way.

c it is more interesting to start sentences with verbs.

4 The procedure gives a set of numbered steps. Could the writer have given any steps in a different order and still been clear? (Give a reason.) ______________________________

____

5 The writer uses precise language to give the instructions. Explain why it was important to tell you:

a that the balloon should be firmly attached. ______________________________

____

b that the surface should be flat and smooth. ______________________________

____

6 a Do you think these instructions were clear and easy to follow? (yes or no) ________

b If you said no, what would have helped you follow them? ______________________________

____

If you said yes, try to make a hovercraft yourself.

Spelling and meaning

hovercraft	cushion	glide	literally	thread
middle	cardboard	exactly	couple	escaping
carefully	attached	surface	usually	moving

1 Write the words in the word box in alphabetical order. Remember: if two words begin with the same letter, put them in order by the second letter. If the second letters are the same, put them in order by the third letter, and so on. When you finish, learn the words using the **look–say–cover–write–check** method.

1. ____________ 2. ____________ 3. ____________

4. ____________ 5. ____________ 6. ____________

7. ____________ 8. ____________ 9. ____________

10. ____________ 11. ____________ 12. ____________

13. ____________ 14. ____________ 15. ____________

Words ending in a **silent e** drop the **e** before adding an ending beginning with a vowel. They keep the e before adding an ending beginning with a consonant.

Examples glide → gliding → glided → glider
move → moving → moved, movement

2 Choose a "silent **e**" word from the box below to write in the sentences. You will need to add ***-ing*** or another ending each time.

divide	make	change	separate	use	face	squeeze	arrange

a Make sure the coloured side is ____________ upwards.

b Stick the wires in, ____________ sure their ends are not touching.

c Keep ____________ the cloth until there is no more liquid left.

d Check the ____________ of the cards to be sure they are equally spaced.

e Draw lines on the paper, ____________ it into twelve equal sections.

f Use staples or glue to stop the pages ____________ at the sides.

g Make different pictures by ____________ the pieces around.

h A knife with a serrated edge would be most ____________.

We often make words by adding two other words together. For example, ***hover*** + ***craft*** makes ***hovercraft***. We call these **compound words**.

3 Draw lines between the words below to make compound words. (You can use a word more than once.)

foot	flake	under	wet	craft	spoon	air
board	water	suit	snow	wear	finger	sun
house	space	print	table	green	proof	ship
word	surf	mill	screen	wind	cross	

Grammar—Verbs and adverbs

You probably know that **verbs** are the words that tell us what someone is doing, saying, thinking, feeling or having.

Procedures mostly use doing or action verbs (underlined) because they show us how to do something.

Examples Carefully stretch the neck of the balloon over the top of the reel.
Let go of the balloon quickly.

Procedures also make use of **adverbs** (circled)—words that tell us **how** to do the actions.

Examples (Carefully) stretch the neck of the balloon over the top of the reel.
Let go of the balloon (quickly.)
Make sure it is (firmly) attached.

Adverbs don't only give information about how. They also give information about where, when and why. Adverbs often end in ***-ly*** but not always. ***Here***, ***yesterday***, ***later*** and ***hard*** are also adverbs.

Underline the verbs in these cooking instructions and circle the adverbs.

a Slice the bread finely to make sandwiches that are easy to eat.

b Cut the sandwiches diagonally so that they look attractive on the plate.

c Heat the frying pan and rub it lightly with butter.

d Divide the mixture evenly into four portions.

e Add all the ingredients and mix them together well.

f Spread the cheese mixture thickly on the bread.

g Leave overnight in a warm place.

Punctuation—Commas to break up clauses

We use **commas to break up sentences with more than one clause**, especially if one clause or the whole sentence is quite long.

Look at these sentences from the text:

Example Glue the reel on top of the CD, so that the hole in the reel lines up exactly with the hole in the CD.
If it doesn't, try giving it a couple of gentle pushes.

The commas help us to understand the ideas in the sentences.

You don't always need commas to separate clauses. The best way to work out if one is needed is to read the sentence out loud. You will often hear if you need a comma.

Can you put commas where they are needed in this procedure? Don't worry if you are not sure about clauses. Just put the commas where you think they will help the reader understand. Remember: reading it out loud will help you.

Easy juggling!

Juggling looks hard but it can be learnt. All you need is three balls and 10 minutes a day for a week to practise.

1

1. Use one ball only and throw it from one hand to the other. Instead of looking at your two hands as you normally would when you throw a ball look at the highest point that the ball reaches. Practise until you feel very comfortable doing this.
2. Using two balls now put one ball in each hand and throw ball 1 from one hand to the other. When ball 1 reaches its highest point throw ball 2. Do not swap ball 2 from one hand to the other but throw it as shown in the drawing. Practise this until you feel comfortable.

2

3

3. Using three balls now do the same as you did in step 2 but this time take two balls in one hand and one ball in the other. Start throwing from the hand with the two balls. Throwing and catching is now a continuous activity. Try to force yourself to throw the balls backwards because otherwise you will throw them forwards and drop them.

Congratulations! You are now juggling!

Can you help?

This student has written clear instructions about how to take a fingerprint, but she has left out the list of things needed. Read the procedure and write the list in the box. Don't forget to give the list a heading. If you like, draw pictures of the things needed.

Be a fingerprint detective!

1. Pour some talcum powder into the saucer.
2. Using the brush, dust some powder lightly onto something hard and shiny that someone has touched —for example, a glass, a windowsill, a doorknob or a mirror.
3. Blow the powder away with a good few blows. You will see some powder left around the fingerprint.
4. Brush the leftover powder lightly with the paintbrush. Use your magnifying glass and you will see the fingerprint gradually appear, as if by magic.

Puzzle time

What am I?

A hovercraft is an unusual kind of transport. Can you work out these other unusual types?

a I am a long narrow boat (rather pretty) pushed along with a pole: G ___ ___ D ___ ___ ___

b I am just a simple seat hanging on a cable: ___ ___ ___ ___ R ___ ___ ___ T

c I am an electric bus that hangs onto overhead wires: T ___ ___ L ___ ___ ___ B ___ ___

d I am in two parts but I go fast on water: C ___ T ___ ___ ___ R ___ ___

e I travel over short distances up and down hills (there is usually one of me going up and another going down): F ___ N ___ ___ ___ L ___ ___

DID YOU KNOW?

Boats of various kinds have been around a long, long time. The oldest boat ever found was a 3-metre long dug-out boat unearthed in the Netherlands. It dated from 7400 BC!

Your turn to write

Tip for crystal-clear writers

When you write a procedure, you need to give clear and precise instructions. For example, instead of writing "Use cardboard", you might write "Use a piece of thin cardboard 10 cm × 10 cm". It is really annoying to read instructions that don't tell you exactly what to do. Don't you agree?

1 The diagrams on the next page show you one way of making paper aeroplanes. (I am sure you have your own favourite way!) Can you write a procedure to go with them? (*Hint:* Get a piece of paper and try to make the aeroplane yourself using the diagrams. This will help you know exactly what to tell your reader and give you ideas for some useful tips to give them.)

Remember:

- Begin with a sentence that tells the aim of the procedure.
- Write a list of the things needed.
- Write clear and precise instructions.
- End with a comment of some kind (congratulations, encouragement or a funny remark).

Be sure to use:

- short, clear sentences
- punctuation and perhaps highlighting to help the reader understand
- command verbs at or near the start of the instruction section
- adverbs to help the reader know how to do the actions
- precise language to show exactly what the reader needs to do.

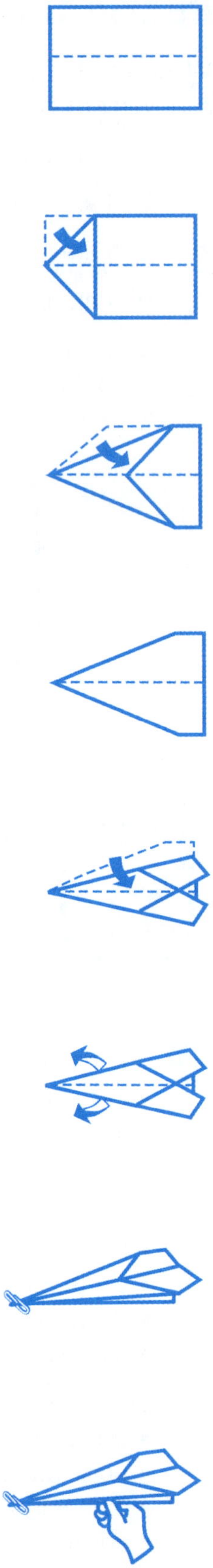

2 Write a procedure for one of these projects. Use the lines below.

- How to plant a small tree or bush
- How to make a campfire
- How to tie your shoelaces (easy to do but very difficult to write!)
- How to take fingerprints
- How to make a kite
- How to catch a fish
- How to do a trick of some kind
- How to make something in the kitchen (e.g. pizza, milkshake, cup of tea)
- How to do a simple science experiment

Use the checklist given for activity 1 and add diagrams to make the instructions clear.

Chapter 5 Writing a letter of request

In a letter of request, your aim is to ask or suggest something in a polite and clear way, and to give your reasons.

STRUCTURE

LANGUAGE

12 KXXXX St
FXXXXXX* NSW
11 March 2004

Mr William Nicholson
c/o Rosemary Cxxxxx
Pxxxxx Fxxxxxx & Dxxxxx
Dxxxx House, 34–43 Rxxxxxx St
London WC2B 5HA

Dear William Nicholson

I have really enjoyed all your books in the series "The Wind on Fire". Thank you very much for writing them. I liked "Slaves of the Mastery" the best! I just couldn't stop reading it till I got to the end, and then I begged my mother to get me the third book, "Firesong".

I was wondering if you would consider writing a fourth book for the series?

I know there might be a few problems in continuing the series because of the way the third book ends. If you are wondering how Kestrel comes back, I've got a good solution. Kestrel's body and spirit come together again through Bowman's love for her. Then Kestrel, Bowman, Mumpo and Pinto (and maybe Sisi) go on another adventure to find a way to get the Singer people back without the Morah coming back too.

PLEASE write a fourth book! I really miss all the characters, especially Bowman and Mumpo.

Thank you

Yours sincerely

Adam Lucas

Adam Lucas

PS I hope you like my drawing.

*We have blocked out the actual addresses for privacy reasons.

Your address and date

Address of person you are writing to

Greeting

***Introduction** to the letter topic*

*Clear **statement of** the letter **purpose***

***Line spaces** between different sections of letter*

***Paragraphs** if needed*

***Ending** —perhaps repeating purpose*

***Sign-off** —showing thanks and respect*

Your name and signature

***PS**—extra comment*

Interesting detail

Polite, respectful language

Personal language

Language to show strength of feeling

Punctuation and highlighting to reinforce feeling

What did you read?

1. Why did Adam write to William Nicholson? ______________________________________

____

2. What is Adam's favourite book in the series? ______________________________
3. Circle the best answer. From what Adam writes, what type of book series do you think The Wind on Fire is?

science fiction	fantasy	adventure	comedy	real life drama	crime

4. Circle the best answer. Adam writes about the characters in the series. He mostly focuses on:
   a what the characters did in the three books in the series.
   b what the characters should have done in the series.
   c what the characters could do in the fourth book.
5. From what Adam writes, what can you work out about what happens at the end of the last book in The Wind on Fire series? ______________________________

____

6. a Have you read any books in The Wind on Fire series? ____________
   b If so, did you like them? Why/Why not? If you have not read them, do you think you would like them, from what Adam writes? Why or why not? ______________________________

____

____

How was it written?

1. Adam's letter is organised in four paragraphs, and each paragraph has a different purpose. Which paragraph:
   a makes his request? _______ b gives suggestions? _______
   c repeats his request? _______ d says which book the letter is about? _______
2. Why do you think that Adam did not make his request right at the start of his letter? ____________

____

3. Adam makes his request very politely (paragraph 2).
   a Underline the seven words he uses to do this.
   b Look at these other ways he could have made his request. Write 1 for the most polite and 3 for the least polite.

   Would you write another book? _____

   Can you write another book? _____

   Would you please write another book? _____

   c Do you think Adam's request was more polite than all of these? (yes or no) ____________

4 Adam makes his letter interesting by giving detail. What detail does he give to show how much he liked the series? ______________________________

5 If you were William Nicholson, would you reply to Adam's letter? Why or why not?

____

Spelling and meaning

wondering	series	really	enjoyed	because
adventure	solution	fourth	couldn't	problems
continuing	through	characters	especially	sincerely

Tip for simply spectacular spellers
If there are words you always spell wrongly (e.g. ***because***), write them in big letters and put them up where you will often see them—for example, next to your bedroom mirror. Choose one or two of the words from the word box to put up by your mirror.

1 When we add ***-ly*** to adjectives ending in ***-al*** or ***-ful*** to make an adverb, we end up with double ***l***, (e.g. ***real*** + ***ly*** → ***really***, ***peaceful*** + ***ly*** → ***peacefully***). Add ***-ly*** to the adjectives in the box and choose one to put in each sentence.

personal	usual	actual	equal	final	annual	general	grateful

a I didn't think I'd like the book at all, but ______________ it was the best book I read this year.

b The boys and girls did ______________ well in the read-a-thon this year.

c I ______________ finished *The Lord of the Rings*. It took me two years.

d That author visits Australia ______________ for the Children's Writing Festival. Last year I heard her speak at the State Library.

e I ______________ read before I go to sleep.

2 Choose words from the word box to complete this student's letter to an author.

I thought the book was the best ______________ I had ever read, ______________ the characters were so lively and interesting. I know there would be some ______________ in writing more books about the same ______________ but one ______________ would be to invent some new ones. I would ______________ like to see Tristan find a new friend to take the place of Joseph. I am not very good at writing so I was ______________ if you could give me some tips when you write back.

3 Here are some words you could use to describe books. Group the words that have similar meaning.

tense moving suspenseful amusing sad frightening hilarious tragic comical funny upsetting humorous mysterious

Grammar—Modals

Sometimes we use special words called **modals** in front of verbs (e.g. ***must***, ***should***, ***ought to***, ***have to***, ***can***, ***could***, ***would***, ***will***, ***may***, ***might***).
We can use modals to show our attitude towards the other person, for example, to show politeness and respect towards people we do not know well or people in authority (e.g. teachers).

Because Adam is requesting something from a famous author he has never met, he writes:
I was wondering if you would consider writing a fourth book for the series?
Would makes his request polite. ***I was wondering*** makes it even more polite.

We also use modals to show how certain we are about something we say.
Examples I know there might be a few problems. (not certain)
I know there will be a few problems. (certain)

We use modals to make requests, unless we know the other person very well. Look at these sentence pairs. Underline which of the two sentences you would use in a letter of request to someone you do not know. Circle the modal that makes the sentence polite. The first has been done for you.

- **a** Write back soon. — (Could) you please write back soon?
- **b** Could you send me a free copy? — Send me a free copy.
- **c** I want to make a suggestion. — May I make a suggestion?
- **d** We all want you to visit our school. — We would all love you to visit our school.
- **e** Your readers want you to keep writing. — Your readers would want you to keep writing.
- **f** You could print more copies of the magazine. — You should print more copies of the magazine.
- **g** Can you please consider my request? — Could you please consider my request?

JOKE

Q. Why do astronauts get a lot of reading done on space missions?
A. They can't put their books down.

Punctuation—Titles and addresses

We use **quotation marks** (**"** ... **"**) for **titles** of books, films, television shows, songs, newspapers, magazines and other published materials.
You can use single (**'** ... **'**) or double (**"** ... **"**) quotation marks, but whichever you choose, you should stick to one method throughout your text. Your teacher might tell you to use one or the other.
If you are typing, you can use *italics* instead of quotation marks for titles. (You can see many examples of this in this book.)

1 Use quotation marks where needed in these sentences. (If ***The*** is part of the title it should be inside the quotation marks.)

a The funniest poem I have heard is a Steven Herrick poem called Science.

b I preferred Blabber Mouth to Worry Warts but Two Weeks with the Queen was my favourite.

c I've read four of Paul Jennings's books: Unreal, Unbelievable, Uncanny and Unbearable.

d At our school we have a poetry competition and last year I recited The Thong.

e I read an extract of The Redback Leftovers by Debra Oswald in The Gazette.

f I watched Around the Twist on television every week when it was on.

When **writing addresses**:
- Use separate lines for the street and the town or suburb.
- Use capital letters to begin names of streets, suburbs, towns, states, countries.
- Write short forms for road, street, avenue, parade, drive, crescent, court, lane and so on (e.g. Rd, St).
- Write the state in capitals and in abbreviated form (e.g. NSW). Write it after the town or suburb, and then add the postcode.
- Write flat or home unit numbers before the street number (e.g. Flat 2, 60 Smith St or 2/60 Smith St).
- Don't use commas or full stops unless you need them to make numbers or words clear.

2 What do these short street forms mean?

Pde ______ Ct ______ Ave ______ St ______

Rd ______ Ln ______ Dr ______ Cr ______

3 Can you write these addresses the right way? (Take a new line for the suburb or town name.)

a 90 valley way flat 2 springfield nsw 2777

______

______

b 356 brighton parade brighton qld 4017

______

______

c 2/6 fletcher st brooklyn tas 7320

______

______

d 623 berry road blackburn vic 3130

______

______

e 23 mill avenue flat 33 fern bay wa 2295

______

______

f 16 bruce crescent dickson act 2602

______

______

Can you help?

This letter of request is to a children's magazine, but the sentences are out of order. Can you number the sentences in the right order, so that Carmen's letter makes sense?

Dear Editor

a _____ My two brothers like the sports section the most because of the interviews with top sports stars, and the competitions.

b _____ I really enjoy the whole magazine, but I especially like the section where you ask readers their opinion on a current issue (News views).

c _____ However, I wondered if you would consider including a book review section where readers write in with their own reviews.

d _____ So please let me know what you think, and thanks for your great magazine.

e _____ I have been getting your magazine *Kidsworld* for a year now.

f _____ I hope you will think hard about my idea. I would be willing to do a book review to get you started. I never stop reading!

g _____ I think your readers would be more interested in reviews written by other kids than in reviews written by adults. Do you think this is a good idea?

Yours sincerely
Carmen Wu

Puzzle time

1 Can you match these authors to their books? You might want to look them up on the Internet to make sure.

Wind in the Willows	Morris Gleitzman
Oliver Twist	Ian Serralier
Matilda	Charles Dickens
Boss of the Pool	Kenneth Grahame
Misery Guts	Norman Lindsay
Animalia	Robin Klein
The Silver Sword	Graeme Base
The Magic Pudding	Roald Dahl

JOKE
Q. What do you get if your postman drops his sack of letters in the dirt?
A. Blackmail.

2 Someone has got these book titles terribly muddled up. Can you write them out the correct way?

Wendy's Adventures in Oz
The Fox the Wizard and the Medicine
The Witch of Wonderland
Peter's Fantastic Wardrobe
Marvellous Mr Lion
George Pan and Alice

Your turn to write

Tip for extraordinary letter writers

When you are writing a letter, be absolutely clear about why you are writing. Then the person is more likely to reply to your letter. Look at the letter Adam received in response to his letter to William Nicholson.*

Dear Adam

Thanks so much for your letter (and the great pictures, especially of dribbly Mumpo). I love it when readers tell me they're enjoying my books. You ask if I could write a fourth book in the Wind on Fire series, but honestly, I can't. The trilogy has come to its natural end, and I do really feel that I can't carry it on beyond that. In a way, I'm pleased when readers get to the end wanting more. So many series of books run out of energy and become boring. But the good news (I hope) is that I'm writing a whole new set of books, called The Noble Warriors. The first book, *Seeker*, is now finished, and should be published next year. I just hope you like it as much, or more, than the trilogy.

All the best from me

William Nicholson

*Printed with permission from William Nicholson

1 Think about a favourite television program that is no longer shown. Use the 'skeleton' letter below to write a letter to the television station asking them to repeat the program. (You address the letter "Dear Sir/Madam", because you don't know the name of the person you are writing to.)

Dear Sir/Madam

I am writing to thank you for showing ______________________________, and

to ask you ______________________________.

I thought that it ______________________________

____

My favourite character/s in the program was/were ______________________________.

I especially loved him/her/them because ______________________________

______________________________.

The best thing about the program was ______________________________

____

____

____

Thank you again for ______________________________. I really hope

____

Yours sincerely

____

2 I am sure you've read many books that you have enjoyed so much that you did not want them to end. Perhaps, like Adam, you have thought about ways for the author to write about the same characters again.

Draft a letter to the author now, using the space below. Follow this pattern:

- Say how much you like the book.
- Clearly state your request to the author.
- Say which characters you would like to see in another book. Say why and, if you can, make some suggestions about how (as Adam did).
- Say something positive and friendly to round off your letter—perhaps repeat your request.
- Sign off your letter in a respectful way.

When you have finished, check your writing for correct grammar, spelling and punctuation, and for polite and respectful language.

3 Write or type your letter out again, and send it off to the publishing company. You can usually find the publisher's address at the front of the book. There is often a publisher's website address as well, and you may even find that you can email your letter to them to send on to the author.

Chapter 6 Giving a factual speech

In a factual speech, your aim is to give your audience information on a topic. However, you should try to make it entertaining as well as informative because you want your audience to listen and take notice of what you are saying.

STRUCTURE

LANGUAGE

Frogs

Good morning 5W. Why is it, do you think, that frogs turn up in so many fairy tales and are hated and feared by beautiful princesses? Well, I think it is because people think frogs are horrible, ugly, slimy little creatures. But actually frogs are quite remarkable, and that is why I want to tell you about them today.

So firstly, what are frogs? Frogs are members of the amphibian class of animals. Amphibians begin life looking like fish and living in water, and then they become adults and live on land.

One of the most interesting things about frogs is their life cycles. Females lay clumps of 2000 to 4000 eggs at a time, and one clump is about the size of a grapefruit. After a few days, the tadpole starts to grow inside the egg. It develops a tail and fins and then, after about 10 days, it emerges from the egg. The tadpole gradually develops limbs and loses its tail, and then lungs replace its gills, allowing it to leave the water and breathe the air.

Frogs eat any animal that moves and is small enough to fit in their mouths—even snakes. And here is something not so nice about frogs. They are cannibals. They eat other frogs, even frogs of their own kind.

You've probably all heard frogs croaking in the garden. But did you know this is really singing? The male frog sings to attract females at breeding time. The female can recognise a male of her kind. She follows his song and finds him in the dark. Very romantic!

We usually think of frogs as the little greenish creatures that we see in our own gardens, but there are many different species of frogs. One interesting example is the Australian water-holding frog which survives drought by making itself a water-filled jacket.

Some frogs are poisonous. The poison arrow frogs of South America are beautiful but deadly. Their bright colours warn their predators of danger. Their poison can paralyse a mammal and can kill a small creature such as a mouse.

So you see—frogs are not uninteresting, ugly little creatures as you may have thought before my talk. They are some of the most fascinating, colourful creatures on earth. Thank you.

Hannah McLean

Structure notes:

Greeting to audience

Introduction to topic and something to capture the audience's interest

Definition of topic (if needed)

Information organised by ***sub-topics***

Not too many details, often just one or two examples

Conclusion which rounds off your talk

Thanks to audience for listening

Language notes:

Questions to involve the audience

Words that show your interest in the topic

Repetition of the topic word to connect ideas

Technical words

Words to show you are about to give some interesting information

Talking directly to the audience to make it more personal

Humour

What did you read?

1. What is special about the amphibian class of animals? ______________________________

____

2. Does a tadpole develop a tail inside the egg or outside? ______________________________

3. What is the last change that happens to frogs before they leave the water? ______________

____

4. Circle the best answer. Male frogs croak:
   - **a** because they cannot sing.
   - **b** because they are thirsty.
   - **c** so that females will find them.

5. What is interesting about the Australian water-holding frog? ______________________

____

6. What is the purpose of the bright colouring of poison arrow frogs? ________________

____

How was it written?

1. The purpose of Hannah's speech was to give information about frogs but she began by talking about frogs in fairytales. Why do you think she did this? ______________________

____

2. Circle the best answer. Why does Hannah define frogs after her introduction?
   - **a** Because it is a basic, important fact about frogs.
   - **b** Because she thought her audience might not have seen a frog.
   - **c** Because she is showing off.

3. If you show you are interested in the topic, your audience will also be interested. Underline the sentences that especially show that Hannah is interested in frogs.

4. Hannah asks her audience many questions to involve them in her talk. Underline all the questions you can find. (These are called **rhetorical** questions.)

5. It can be a good idea to help your audience understand new information by relating it to everyday things. What does Hannah compare a clump of eggs to (paragraph 3)? ________________

6. Hannah clearly divides up her speech into five sub-topics. In which order does she talk about them?

   diet ___ mating habits ___ poisonous frogs ___ life cycle ___ different species ___

7. What three words in the last paragraph tell the audience that Hannah is about to end her speech?

   ______ ______ ______

JOKE

Q. Where do frogs fly their flags?

A. On the tadpole.

Spelling and meaning

beautiful	horrible	creatures	remarkable	amphibian
cycle	develops	emerges	gradually	cannibals
probably	romantic	species	interesting	poisonous

Tip for sensational spellers

When learning difficult words, underline the hard part and study it for a while, saying the troublesome letters out loud again and again. For example, you might underline the ***eau*** in beautiful and say ***e–a–u***, ***e–a–u***, ***e–a–u***.

1. Look at the words in the word box and underline the hardest parts for you. Then learn the words using the **look–say–cover–write–check** method.

2. Now try to fill in the missing letters below WITHOUT LOOKING BACK. (Warning! The hardest bits have been left out.) Check your answers by looking at the word box.

b ___ ___ ___ tiful	ho ___ ___ ible	creat ___ ___ es	remark ___ ble	am ___ ___ ibian
c ___ cle	devel ___ ps	em ___ ___ ___ es	grad ___ ___ lly	cann ___ b ___ ls
prob ___ ___ ly	roman ___ ___ ___	spe ___ ___ ___ s	int ___ ___ esting	poison ___ ___ s

3. We make many adjectives by adding endings (suffixes) to base words (e.g. ***poison*** + ***ous*** = ***poisonous***). Can you match the base words in the box and the endings in the oval to make descriptive adjectives?

danger	interest
grace	dead
power	live
colour	astonish
green	

ing, ful, ful, ly, ful, ing, ly, ous, ish

_______________ _______________ _______________

_______________ _______________ _______________

_______________ _______________ _______________

4. Choose a word from the word box to put in the sentences below.

   a Animals who eat members of their own species are _______________.

   b Toads, frogs and salamanders are all _______________.

   c The adult silkworm moth _______________ from its cocoon after about three weeks.

   d 'Toxic' is another word for _______________.

   e I think penguins are the most beautiful _______________ on the planet.

   f Over the next few months, the bear cub _______________ learns to find food for itself.

Grammar—Compound sentences

Sometimes we can't say all that we want to in a simple sentence (one subject and one verb). When we have two or more ideas that are equally important to say in one sentence, we can combine them to make a **compound sentence**.

A compound sentence has two or more **independent clauses** (clauses that make sense by themselves). Compound sentences are usually joined with ***and***, ***but*** or ***or***.

Examples Females lay clumps of eggs (clause 1), and one clump is about the size of a grapefruit (clause 2).

A tadpole looks like a fish (clause 1) but it is not one (clause 2).

If the subject of the clauses is the same, we can use a pronoun instead of a noun in the second clause.

Example **Frogs** might be very plain or ***they*** might be brightly coloured. (***they*** is used instead of ***frogs***)

Or we can leave the subject out altogether in the second clause.

Example **She** follows his song and finds him in the dark. (We know the subject of the second clause is ***she***.)

Draw lines to make compound sentences from the clauses on the left and those on the right. Use the conjunctions in the middle to connect them.

1 Tadpoles feed mainly on algae.	and	a	He keeps them at the correct temperature until ready to hatch.
2 The male toad protects the eggs from predators.	but	b	It must come to the surface every now and then to breathe air.
3 The frill-necked lizard usually keeps its frill folded flat.	and	c	They will sometimes tackle an insect swimming in the water.
4 The frill-necked lizard is exceptionally fast moving on the ground.	but	d	It mostly runs upright on its hind legs.
5 Green turtles used to be common in warm oceans.	but	e	Today their numbers are a fraction of what they once were.
6 The green turtle is most at home underwater.	but	f	It will raise it during courtship or when threatened.

Punctuation—Highlighting

When you write out your speech, it is a good idea to **highlight** some words (e.g. by underlining or writing in capitals). This will remind you which words to emphasise or say with special expression. The best way to find out which words to highlight is to read your speech out loud beforehand. Full stops, commas, exclamation marks and question marks also help you deliver a speech smoothly. For example, they tell you when to pause, when to look up at the audience, and when to change your voice in some way.

Look at the words Hannah underlined at the beginning of her speech.

> Good morning 5W. Why is it, do you think, that frogs turn up in so many fairy tales and are hated and feared by beautiful princesses? Well, I think it is because people think frogs are horrible, ugly, slimy little creatures. But actually frogs are quite remarkable, and that is why I want to tell you about them today.

Now underline the words you would emphasise in the section of her speech below. Read it out loud to help you.

Frogs eat any animal that moves and is small enough to fit in their mouths—even snakes. And here is something not so nice about frogs. They are cannibals. They eat other frogs, even frogs of their own kind.

You've probably all heard frogs croaking in the garden. But did you know this is really singing? The male frog sings to attract females at breeding time. The female can recognise a male of her kind. She follows his song and finds him in the dark. Very romantic!

Can you help?

These students are trying to decide which way to start their speeches. Can you help them choose the best sentences to capture their audience's attention? Number the sentences 1, 2 and 3 in order from most interesting to least interesting. (There is no definite right answer—it is your opinion.)

1 For a speech about the Siberian tiger:

___ Did you know that there are only 200 Siberian tigers left in the wild?

___ Siberian tigers are very beautiful and very rare.

___ The Siberian tiger is the largest cat in the whole world.

2 For a speech about orang-utans:

___ The orang-utan is the second largest primate.

___ In the Malay language, "orang" means "man" and "utan" means "jungle", so "orang-utan" means "man of the jungle".

___ The orang-utan is only found in Sumatra and Borneo.

3 For a speech about the clownfish:

___ The common clownfish lives on Australia's Great Barrier Reef.

___ Did you see the movie *Finding Nemo*?

___ The clownfish gets its name from its white bands, which look like circus face paint.

Puzzle time

Can you work out these animal words? Add one letter to the word and then rearrange it to make the name of an animal. Use the clues to help you. For example, FOR (likes to croak) → Answer: FROG (FOR + G).

a RED (Bambi was one of these) __________

b LOW (likes to howl at night) __________

c SOME (has very large antlers) __________

d ROSE (a friend to humans) __________

e TIRE (don't go too close) __________

f RASH (very sharp teeth) __________

g HEAL (rather large) __________

h LAME (a good traveller) __________

Your turn to write

Tips for stupendous speakers

- Write your speech on small cards.
- Look up from your cards as much as you can.
- Make eye contact with different people in the audience.
- Pause often to give your audience time to catch up. It is a good idea to write "STOP!" in big letters on your cards after every few lines.
- Speak loudly and clearly. Imagine you are speaking to the person at the back of the room.
- Try not to be nervous. Smile at your audience. They will usually smile back and you will immediately feel better.

1 In the box below are some facts about the size and power of the Siberian tiger. Can you link them up into a paragraph to use in a speech?
- Write a sentence to introduce the topic (tiger's size and power).
- Leave out detail or change words if you want.
- Add your own ideas to make the information interesting (e.g. compare size to something the audience will understand).
- Mention any personal experiences (e.g. seeing a Siberian tiger in the zoo).
- Add a personal comment.
- Underline the words you would emphasise or say with special expression.

- Largest cat in world: 1.05–1.10 metres tall, 1.4–2.8 metres long
- Very heavy: 180–306 kilograms (the heaviest tiger on record was 383 kilograms)
- Very strong: can drag prey that would take twelve men to move
- Excellent hearing and vision: can see over five times better than humans at night
- Long, sharp claws that spring out when hunting

2 Some information about the Komodo dragon is shown on the next page. Not all the information is important or interesting.

- [ ] Class of animal: reptile
- [ ] Officially named in 1912
- [ ] 2.8 metres long (longer than a small car); tail half its length
- [ ] 30–60 kilograms
- [ ] Largest land lizard
- [ ] Breeding season: June or July
- [ ] Lays up to 20 eggs
- [ ] Incubation: 8–8.5 months
- [ ] Lifespan: 30 years
- [ ] Young have black and green stripes on neck
- [ ] Lives on Indonesian islands
- [ ] Islands include Komodo, Rintja, Padar, Flores, Gili Mota and Oewada Sami
- [ ] Criminals used to be taken to the islands and left to defend themselves against the dragons
- [ ] Can't breathe fire like an imaginary dragon but can hiss and flick its forked tongue very frighteningly
- [ ] Uses tongue to 'taste' the air and know if prey are about
- [ ] Eats anything it can find—size does not matter; eats wild pig, deer, monkey
- [ ] Can eat most of a deer in one go
- [ ] Population is stable. Because it lives on uninhabited islands, it is in no danger from humans but is vulnerable because it has a very limited habitat
- [ ] Very fast, can outpace a human in thick vegetation; can move fast in water too
- [ ] Ambushes prey, grips it in its powerful jaws and claws, tears it apart

a Can you tick ten facts that would be suitable for a two-minute speech (350 words). Choose only the facts that are very important or that the audience will find interesting.

b Now draft your speech, using the following lines. Change the words as you need to, to make your speech clear and interesting.

Introduction to capture audience interest (e.g. a question to the audience, a very interesting fact)

Definition or classification of the animal

Information about animal organised by sub-topics (e.g. appearance, diet, habitat)

Ending (e.g. a comment, a warning)

3 If you wish, choose an animal you are especially interested in, and write a two-minute speech about it. You will have to do your own research for this task, but don't make your job too big. Remember, you will only have time to cover a few interesting areas and give a few examples.

- Follow the pattern suggested in activity 2.
- Use your Writer's Notebook to write a draft of your speech. If you are going to deliver your speech, write it out again on small cards. Highlight words that need emphasis, and use punctuation to help you deliver the speech smoothly.

Answers on pages 95–96

Chapter 7 Writing an explanation

The aim of an explanation is to tell how or why something happens. Explanations are often about natural or scientific phenomena, processes or events.

STRUCTURE

LANGUAGE

Carnivorous plants

These students wrote their explanations after watching a video about carnivorous (flesh-eating) plants. These plants live in places that have very few nutrients in the soil. To survive in this hostile environment, they capture and eat live prey. Most eat insects, but some can swallow rats and small birds.

Venus Flytrap

The Venus Flytrap is an extraordinary plant. It is a carnivorous (flesh-eating) plant which can digest flies and other insects.

When the 'trap' is open, it looks like a large seashell with sharp, spiky 'teeth'. It has bright colours and a beautiful scent.

Insects are attracted to the plant because of its vibrant colours and its sweet-scented nectar. The insects land on the small 'trigger' hairs of the trap and this pressure causes the trap to close. If the insect is too small, the chamber will not close, because there is not enough pressure. Once the trap has swallowed an insect it takes ten days to digest it.

The Venus Flytrap prefers tropical weather and so it is found in places like South America. It is often used by people to catch the annoying insects that fly around their houses. In my opinion it's a very useful plant!

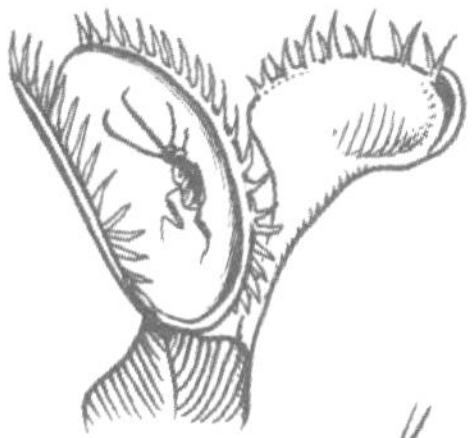

Bradley Aldous

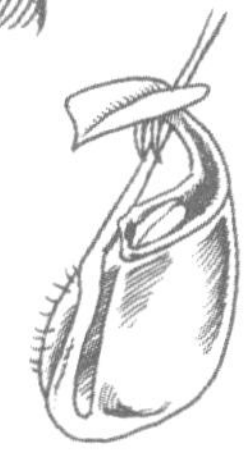

The Pitcher of Death

You may have heard of a plant called the Pitcher of Death. As you can probably tell by its name, it kills and eats insects. If you want to know how, read on!

To catch flies and other insects, this plant needs a bait and a trap. The bait in this case is nectar. The trap is the cup or 'pitcher' shaped leaves which have short hairs at the top to give the insect a sure foothold, but slippery hairs pointing downwards, so it can't escape once it falls in. The other part of the trap is a digestive fluid inside the cup.

How it catches the insect is really quite simple. First the insect is attracted by the nectar. Then it slips on the smooth inner surface of the plant. Next it is forced downwards by the slippery hairs. Then it falls into the digestive fluid and is drowned.

An interesting fact about this plant is that the pitcher leaves can grow to the size of a fully grown adult's hand.

Erin Allen

Statement to identify the phenomenon (often a definition or classification)

Features of the phenomenon (not always)

Paragraphs explaining the phenomenon

Explanation given in order that things happen

Additional information or concluding statement (not always)

Mainly factual information

Technical words—often with everyday explanations

Clauses beginning with *so, because, when, if*

Usually **present tense verbs**

Time words

Some passive voice

Compound and complex sentences

What did you read?

1. A carnivorous plant is a ________________ plant. They mostly eat ________________.
2. Circle the best answer. Why have some plants become carnivorous?
   - a Because they need nutrients which their environment can't provide
   - b Because they want to stop their predators eating them
   - c Because they are greedy
3. What attracts insects to both the Venus Flytrap and the Pitcher of Death? ________________
4. What triggers the 'trap' in the Venus Flytrap to close? ________________

   Does the trap close for all insects? ________________
5. In the end what causes the death of the insect in the Pitcher of Death? ________________

   ____
6. The Pitcher of Death allows the insect to get a sure foothold at the start. Why do you think this is important? ________________

How was it written?

1. Both students tell us exactly what they are explaining in the ________________ sentence of their text.
2. Both students also tell us that the plant eats and kills insects. Which student relates this to the definition of carnivorous? ________________
3. Bradley compares the plant to something else. What? ________________

   Why does he do this? ________________

   ____
4. You often need to identify the features of the thing you are writing about before you explain how it works. Which features does Bradley identify? ________________
5. It is important to explain how things happen in the order that they happen. Can you sort out the right order for these events and put them under the right plant heading?
   - Insects land on trap
   - Insects digested
   - Insects attracted by nectar and colour
   - Insects fall into digestive fluid and drown
   - Trap closes
   - Insects slip on smooth surface
   - Insects attracted by nectar
   - Insects forced down by slippery hairs
   - Insects digested

Venus Flytrap	**Pitcher of Death**
________________	________________
________________	________________
________________	________________
________________	________________
	________________

6. a Did you think the students' explanations were clear? ________________

   b Is there anything you needed more information about? ________________

Spelling and meaning

nutrients	hostile	extraordinary	flies	insects
digest	spiky	scent	vibrant	pressure
chamber	swallowed	pitcher	slippery	fluid

1 Choose a word from the word box to place in these sentences. Then learn all the words in the box using the **look–say–cover–write–check** method.

a The birds attract their partners with their ________________ colouring.

b Every living thing seeks out the things that will give it the ________________ to survive.

c ________________ is another word for unfriendly.

d Some carnivorous animals can ________________ small animals such as rats and birds.

e The ________________ of flowers plays an important role in plant reproduction.

f A ________________ can be a small enclosed space, or a large room or hall.

g A ________________ is the same as a jug and quite different from a 'picture'.

h There can be enough ________________ in some pitcher plants to drown a small frog.

Adding endings to words that end in ***y*** can be tricky. Here are the most important rules.

- Keep the ***y*** when adding ***ing*** to words ending in ***y***. This keeps the two ***i*** sounds—one long, one short (e.g. fl***ying***, sta***ying***, marr***ying***).
- Keep the ***y*** when adding any endings to words that end in a **vowel +*y*** (e.g. prey → pre***ys***, destroy → destro***yed***).
- Change the ***y*** to ***i*** when adding endings to words that end in a **consonant +*y*** (e.g. fly → fl***ies***, marry → marr***ies***, marr***iage***).

2 Add the endings to these words following the rules.

a prey + ing ________________

b slippery + ness ________________

c beauty + ful ________________

d extraordinary + ly ________________

e easy + ly ________________

f hurry + ed ________________

g spiky + ness ________________

h carry + ing ________________

i annoy + ing ________________

j enjoy + ed ________________

3 We often make new words by adding endings to others (sometimes changing one or more letters). Use all or part of a word in the word box to make these new words.

a eating well: ___ ___ ___ ___ ition

b the process of food going down: ___ ___ ___ ___ ___ ___ ion

c something to kill creepy-crawlies: ___ ___ ___ ___ ___ ___ icide

d the opposite of friendliness: ___ ___ ___ ___ ___ ___ ity

e wateriness: ___ ___ ___ ___ ___ ity

f liveliness: ___ ___ ___ ___ ___ ___ cy

4 Brad calls the Venus Flytrap ***extraordinary*** meaning "very special" or "out of the ordinary". Can you work out these synonyms for ***extraordinary***? (Remember, synonyms are words with similar meanings.)

a ___ ___ AZ ___ ___ ___
b ___ ___ SCIN ___ ___ ING
c ___ ___ CREDI ___ ___ ___
d ___ ___ BEL ___ ___ ___ AB ___ ___
e AS ___ ___ NISH ___ ___ ___
f REM ___ ___ ___ AB ___ ___

Grammar—Complex sentences

Sometimes we want to say something that is too complicated to be said in a simple or a compound sentence. We need a **complex sentence**.

A complex sentence has:

- one **main or independent clause** that makes sense by itself
- at least one other clause that gives detail about the main clause and is **dependent** on it to make sense.

In these sentences from the text, notice how the main clauses (underlined) could be sentences by themselves:

> When the 'trap' is open, it looks like a large seashell with sharp, spiky 'teeth'.
> If you want to know how, read on!
> If the insect is too small, the chamber will not close, because there is not enough pressure.

In the sentences above, the dependent clauses add extra detail about the verbs in the main clauses: about if, when, where, why or how. They are **adverbial clauses**. An adverbial clause needs the main clause to make a sentence.

1 Underline the main clauses in these sentences.

a Insects are attracted to it because of the vibrant colours and sweet-scented nectar.
b Once the trap has swallowed an insect, it takes ten days to digest it.
c As you can probably tell by its name, it kills and eats insects.
d To catch flies and other insects, this plant needs a bait and a trap.

2 Match these main clauses and adverbial clauses so they make the best sense. Draw lines between the matching clauses.

Main clause

a People don't often keep this plant in the house
b You should really watch your step
c The fly gets stuck
d The plant eats the flies and insects
e Venus Flytraps sometimes catch and eat small frogs

Adverbial clause

i when it lands.
ii because it doesn't get nitrogen from the soil.
iii although they are not designed for large prey.
iv if you live in Malaysia!
v because it can be deadly.

3 Look at the clauses below. Write **I** if the clause could exist as a sentence by itself. Write **D** if it needs another clause to make sense.

a Carnivorous plants are very widespread in nature. ___
b When trigger hairs near the entrance are touched. ___
c Some have bright colours. ___
d While the adults have no trouble flying in and out. ___
e The spider is a regular dweller in pitcher plants. ___
f Because the trigger sets off an electrical charge. ___

Punctuation—It's and its

It's and ***its*** are easy to confuse, but just remember these two things:
- ***It's*** ALWAYS, ALWAYS, ALWAYS means "it is" or (less commonly) "it has".
- ***Its*** is a word meaning "belonging to it" (just like ***hers*** means "belonging to her")

Examples In my opinion it's a very useful plant! (It is a very useful plant!)
It's been known to eat small birds. (It has been known to eat small birds.)
Insects are attracted to the plant because of its vibrant colours. (... the vibrant colours of it)

So, only use ***it's***, if you can replace it with ***it is*** or ***it has*** and the sentence still makes sense.

Fill in the blanks with ***it's*** or ***its***. Remember, only use ***it's***, if you can replace it with ***it is*** or ***it has***.

a The sun is the basis of life on our planet. __________ rays give us heat and light.

b The shape of a flower usually tells us how __________ pollinated.

c A honey bee might flap __________ wings 200 times per second when in flight.

d When a worker bee finds a good source of nectar, it returns to __________ hive to let other workers know.

e __________ fascinating to study how bees communicate with each other using dance.

Can you help?

This explanation makes sense but the writer has forgotten to use capital letters, full stops and commas. Can you help put them in the right place? Reading the explanation out loud will help.

How coral reefs form

the great barrier reef is the largest living structure on earth and is even visible from space most people know this reef is made of coral but many people do not know how coral reefs form coral reefs look like rocks but they are actually animals the reefs are made up of colonies of tiny creatures called polyps these polyps produce limestone from their outer cells the limestone gradually builds up around them making them larger and larger every year as the polyps reproduce and new polyps grow the reef expands each polyp is connected to its neighbours by strands of living tissues and this is how the polyps make up a whole reef

JOKE
Q. What do you call an insect that goes in your ear?
A. A space invader.

Puzzle time

What am I? I am a kind of plant ...

a I have been around for millions of years. I am rather short—no more than 3 centimetres. I like rather humid, moist conditions. I begin with M and end with S. I am ___ ___ ___ ___.

b I reproduce by spores, not seeds. I usually have a curly kind of shape. Like M above I have a long history on Earth, and I also like humid, moist conditions. One of my type is the national plant of New Zealand. I begin with F and end with N. I am a ___ ___ ___ ___.

c We are a very primitive life form. We usually live in water. We can be single cell or complicated multi-cell organisms such as seaweed. We can cause big problems for humans and other animal life. At the moment one of our type is creating trouble in the Great Barrier Reef. We begin with A and end with E. We are ___ ___ ___ ___ ___ .

d I am a strange member of the plant kingdom. I can't use energy from the sun to produce nutrients (food) for myself, so I have to feed on dead material or another living organisms. Some of my type are poisonous---even deadly. Some are very nice to eat. Some of us are extremely colourful. I begin with F and end with S. I am a ___ ___ ___ ___ ___ ___.

Your turn to write

Tip for seriously smashing writers

When writing an explanation, it helps to make a plan first. Jot down all the information your readers will need to really understand. Put the information in the order that will help them most.

1 Use the diagrams and information in the box to write an explanation on the scaffold on the next page about how spiders make their webs. Add your own words and ideas to make the explanation interesting and easy to understand.

- Spiders' webs made from silk—silk very important for survival
- Silk made in glands in abdomen—silk very strong
- Liquid when it comes out—turns solid in air—can't dissolve in water
- Many different kinds of webs—wheel-shaped web most common—also funnel-shaped, dome-shaped, bell-shaped ones—no two spider webs the same

Step 1: straight horizontal line

Step 2: Y shape—bottom of Y anchored to branch or other object

Step 3: spokes of wheel—attached to branch or other object

Step 4: makes circular scaffold starting in centre—dry, non-sticky silk so spider can walk on it

Step 5: works back from edge to centre—replaces non-sticky with sticky silk—silk tied to each spoke

Spider waits in centre—leg on a strand—feels insect, moves quickly to search for it

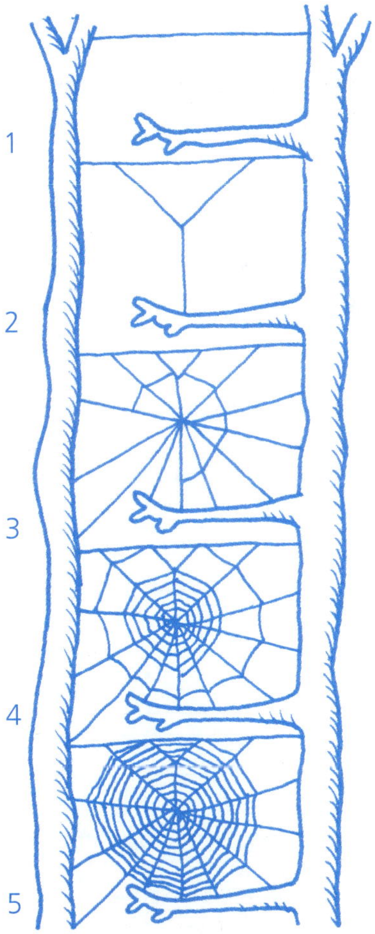

Title ______

Statement about phenomenon (e.g. where silk comes from) ______

Features (e.g. types of webs) ______

Explanation of phenomenon (in order it happens) ______

Concluding statement

2 For extra practice, write an explanation of one of the natural phenomena in the box below, using your Writer's Notebook.

- Do some research to find out how the phenomenon occurs or works.
- Write a plan that includes all the important things you need to mention.
- Draft your explanation following the stages in activity 1 above.
- Read through your explanation as you go to make sure it is clear and makes sense.
- Proofread for spelling and punctuation.
- When you finish your draft give it to someone else to read. Make changes if they did not understand something or if you left out important information.
- Write your explanation out properly on your own paper.
- Draw a picture to go with it.

How do flying fish fly?
How does a chameleon change colour?
How do fish breathe?
How can an owl see at night?
How does a caterpillar become a butterfly?
How do birds know when to migrate?

DID YOU KNOW?

A house fly lives for fourteen days—unless it gets eaten first by a Venus Flytrap!

Answers on page 96

Chapter 8 Writing a review

The aim of a review is to give your readers information about a book, play or film and your opinion of it overall.

STRUCTURE

LANGUAGE

Tom Jones saves the world, by Steven Herrick

Tom Jones Saves the World is a very funny verse novel about families, friendship and forgiveness by well-known poet and author Steven Herrick. It tells the tale of Thomas Wilbur Johannes Harold Jones, who desperately wants to have an exciting life like the kids he reads about in books.

Tom has moved with his mother and father to Pacific Palms. He thinks it is "a prison for kids" because it has a wall right around it and can only be entered by a massive iron security gate and with a PIN number. He is driven mad by his father's obsessions with his new job and his bottle top collection (taking up three rooms of the house). He hates the safe, lonely, boring life of Pacific Palms. He yearns for his old life when he could go down to the creek and catch yabbies, walk down to the shops and know everybody, and play cricket with his dad in the backyard.

His feelings towards his parents and his new life start to change when he discovers a surprising secret about his mum, Barbara. Shortly afterwards, he meets his old Grandpa Jones for the first time and finds out why he and his dad have not spoken for years. Then he meets Cleo (short for Cleopatra). Cleo longs to have normal parents with boring lives. Instead, her parents are archeologists who are always away in strange countries "digging up ancient bits of rubbish" and leaving her with her aunt and uncle in Pacific Palms.

Cleo is a girl with lots of bright ideas. One idea is to build a secret escape hatch from Pacific Palms. The novel follows Tom's adventures with Cleo outside the wall, and their attempts to get his dad and his grandpa back together again.

Tom Jones Saves the World made me laugh out loud in places and get a lump in my throat in others. I loved all the main characters—even Tom's funny old dad, Arnold. I liked the way the story was told in verse. Somehow this pushed me onwards to the next page, and then the next, until suddenly I was on the last page. I think this book will appeal to a very broad range of readers because of Steven Herrick's wicked humour, but I particularly recommend it for children between the ages of 11 and 14 (and their parents!).

Introduction identifies the book, author, type of book and what it is about (theme)

Description of the book: setting, characters and main events in plot

Paragraphs

Comment on author's writing style

Judgment: your opinion and a recommendation

Words that show your opinion

Mostly **present tense**

Adjectives to describe action and characters

Short quotations from book to give example of author's style

Thinking and feeling verbs

What did you read?

1. What are the themes of *Tom Jones Saves the World?* (What is it about?) (three words)

____________ ____________ ____________

2. The novel is written in the form of a poem. Which word tells you this? ____________

3. a Name one thing that Tom does not like about his life in Pacific Palms. ____________

____

   b Name one thing he liked about his old life. ____________

____

4. True or false?
   a Tom's father has never spent time playing with him. ______
   b Tom has never met his Grandpa Jones before. ______
   c Cleo would like boring parents just like Tom's. ______
   d *Tom Jones Saves the World* is sad as well as funny. ______

5. Why do you think Cleo was named after Cleopatra? (The review gives us a hint but does not tell us exactly.) ____________

6. If you have read this book, do you agree with the reviewer? Why or why not? If you have not read the book, would you like to now, based on this review? Why or why not?

____

____

____

How was it written

1. The review is organised in paragraphs. Draw lines to match the paragraphs to what they tell us.

Paragraph 1	some of the most important events of the plot
Paragraph 2	the reviewer's overall opinion
Paragraph 3	the story setting and the main character
Paragraph 4	how the story develops
Paragraph 5	the name of the book, its author and its theme

2. The reviewer mentions many of the characters but gives most detail about ____________ and ____________, because they are the main characters.

3. The reviewer does not tell us how the story ends. Why? ____________

____

4. *Tom Jones Saves the World* is full of interesting and amusing events and experiences. The reviewer only mentions the most I __ __ __ __ __ __ __ T.

5. A review often ends with a R __ __ __ MM __ __ __ ATION to readers. Underline this part of the review.

Spelling and meaning

theme	verse	novel	friendship	forgiveness
author	desperately	obsession	yearns	attempts
characters	wicked	humour	particularly	recommend

1 Synonyms are words that have similar meanings. Can you write a synonym from the word box for these words?

a advise ____________________

b passion ____________________

c comedy ____________________

d especially ____________________

e efforts ____________________

f writer ____________________

g story book ____________________

h poetry ____________________

i topic ____________________

j very much ____________________

k wants very much ____________________

l reconciliation ____________________

m naughty ____________________

n relationship ____________________

o people ____________________

2 Here are some synonyms for ***funny***, but the letters are muddled up. Can you sort them out?

a MUINGAS ____________________

b OUSMUHRO ____________________

c LHIRASIOU ____________________

d TTWIY ____________________

e OMCLAIC ____________________

3 You usually mention some of the things below when writing a review. Can you complete the words? (Two words are from the word box. You can find some others by the side of the review.)

a ___ L ___ T

b ___ H ___ ___ A ___ T ___ RS

c T ___ ___ ME

d DI ___ LO ___ UE

e ___ CT ___ ___ N

f AT ___ ___ ___ PH ___ RE

g S ___ TT ___ ___ G

h ILL ___ ___ T ___ AT ___ ___ NS

i L ___ ___ OUT

j L ___ NG ___ ___ GE

k WRITING ___ T ___ LE

4 Cleo's parents are ***archaeologists***. They study objects (usually buried) that were used by people in the past. The ending ***-ologist*** means "person who studies something". Do you know what these ***-ologists*** study?

a Marine biologist: S ___ ___ A ___ ___ ___ ___ LS

b Geologist: R ___ ___ KS

c Entomologist: I ___ ___ ___ ___ TS

d Paleontologist: F ___ ___ ___ ILS

Grammar—Adjectives

We use **adjectives** to give extra information about a noun. For example:

- what it is made of (***plastic***, ***paper***, ***wooden***)
- what size it is (***big***, ***massive***, ***small***)
- what shape it is (***round***, ***oblong***, ***triangular***)
- what it is like (***exciting***, ***boring***, ***wet***, ***dry***)

Usually the adjective comes before the noun (e.g. He has an exciting life.), but sometimes it comes after a being verb (e.g. His life is exciting.).

Two important types of adjectives are factual adjectives and opinion adjectives. **Factual adjectives** describe something in an objective way—they give information that can be proved somehow. If you say a story is "short", this could be proved by counting the pages.

Opinion adjectives give someone's opinion of something. For example, one person might say a story is "interesting", and another might say it is "boring". There is no way to prove which is right.

1 Underline the adjectives in these sentences. Write **F** if the adjective is a factual adjective and **O** if the adjective is an opinion adjective.

a The tiny creature ends up saving all the children. _____
b The book tells the tale of an imaginary tribe who lived 3000 years ago. _____
c The film was confusing because there were so many characters. _____
d The story is set in a magical land beyond the North Pole. _____
e The story takes place in a haunted house. _____
f The ending of the film was so terrifying, I could not watch. _____

2 Reviews mainly use opinion adjectives. Look at the opinion adjectives in the box. Write each one next to an opinion adjective below with a similar meaning.

weird	action-packed	tense	extraordinary	sad	believable
fascinating	light-hearted	magical	unbelievable	wacky	monotonous

a moving ____________________
b humorous ____________________
c fast-paced ____________________
d bizarre ____________________
e zany ____________________
f realistic ____________________
g incredible ____________________
h unusual ____________________
i fantastic ____________________
j intriguing ____________________
k suspenseful ____________________
l dull ____________________

Punctuation—Apostrophe of possession

We use an **apostrophe** to show that a person or thing **owns or possesses** another.

Examples Tom's father (the father of Tom)
the book's ending (the ending of the book)

People often get confused about when and where to use the apostrophe of possession, but it is really very simple.

When to use it

You only use the apostrophe when one person or thing **owns** another.

Examples Tom took his Grandpa's hand. (**Right:** Grandpa owns his hand, so you need an apostrophe.)

Tom has two Grandpa's. (**Wrong:** Grandpa owns nothing, so you don't need an apostrophe.)

Tom has two Grandpas. (**Right:** "Grandpas" is simply plural.)

Where to put it

You only have to remember *one* thing about where to put the apostrophe of possession.

Put the apostrophe immediately after the person or thing that does the possessing.

Examples

Tom's house = the house of <u>Tom</u> → apostrophe goes after <u>Tom</u> → Tom's

My parents' house = the house of my <u>parents</u> → apostrophe goes after <u>parents</u> → parents'

The children's house = the house of the <u>children</u> → apostrophe goes after <u>children</u> → children's

That's it! No need to think about singulars and plurals. Just ask yourself who or what does the owning and *then* put the apostrophe.

1 Put the apostrophes where needed in these sentences. (One is needed in each sentence.)

- **a** Harry Potters friends were Hermione and Ron.
- **b** The book tells the story of the womens struggle for freedom.
- **c** The teachers staffroom is the last place Bill wants to be at lunchtime.
- **d** The mouses tail gets chopped off quite early in the story.
- **e** The sword becomes the symbol of the childrens quest.
- **f** The boys terrible argument leads to disaster.

2 Put the apostrophes where needed in these sentences. (Some sentences don't need any.)

- **a** Many readers will find the story difficult to follow.
- **b** None of Miras classmates will speak to her.
- **c** Jason believes the neighbours might be aliens.
- **d** The twins inheritance changes their lives.
- **e** His little sisters diary reveals the horrible truth.
- **f** Hank desperately wants to play in the mens soccer team.

REMINDER!

You always have to indicate titles of books, films and plays in some way. If you are typing, you can use *italics*, but if not, use inverted commas (" … ") or <u>underlining</u>.

Can you help?

Can you help this student punctuate his short review of the film *Harry Potter and the Prisoner of Azkaban*? Use underlining for the film title and remember to use apostrophes to show possession. Put a / where you think a new paragraph would start.

harry potter and the prisoner of azkaban is the third film of the harry potter book series by j k rowling like the earlier films it takes us into the magical world of harry and his two trusted friends ron and hermione this film finds harry and his friends in their third year at hogwarts a serial killer sirius black has escaped from the wizard prison azkaban sirius was the friend of harrys parents who gave them up to lord voldemort everyone believes that sirius is now after harry I enjoyed this film more than the two earlier ones because it was much scarier I also liked the new characters such as sirius black and professor lupin however there were parts of the book left out that I thought were important to include for example the connection between harrys father sirius and professor lupin the special effects were as brilliant as ever if you are a harry potter fan you must not miss harry potter and the prisoner of azkaban

Puzzle time

These well-known books and films have been rewritten using different words. Can you work them out using the letters given?

a Visually unattractive young bird: T □□ U □□□ D □□□□□□□

b Stellar conflict: S □□□ W □□□

c Breeze in the trees by the river: W □□□ I □ T □□ W □□□□□□

d Housed in isolation: H □□□ A □□□□

e Disgusting verse: R □□□□□□□□ R □□□□□

f The confused marsupial: □□□ M □□□□□□-H □□□□□ W □□□□□

g Amazing sly dog of the male gender: F □□□□□□□□ M □ F □□

h Marsupial wizardry: P □□□□□ M □□□□

i Pure and pale meets seven vertically challenged men: S □□□ W □□□□ A □□ T □□ S □□□□ D □□□□□□

Your turn to write

Tips for red-hot reviewers

- Don't get bogged down telling the whole story of the book—just mention the main events. And definitely don't give the ending away!
- Don't be tempted to copy the words from the blurb at the back of the book.
- Look up the Internet for information about authors and their books. You will find out all sorts of information. Try Steven Herrick to start with.

1 Think about a book you could review now (perhaps one you have read recently). Prepare for writing by making notes about the book on the lines below. The questions are meant as prompts—you might not have something to say for each. Use point form—don't write in full sentences.

Name of book ______________________________

Author ______________________________

What type of book is it (e.g. fantasy, real-life drama, spy, detective, family story, comedy, adventure, romance, verse, mystery, comic-book—or maybe a combination)? ______________________________

____

Can you identify a theme (e.g. families, friendship, independence, prejudice, love, war)?

____

Where and when is the story set? What is interesting about this?

Who are the main characters? What is interesting about them (e.g. sad, funny, irritating)? Are they realistic?

What are the important events in the story, especially those that set up the main action?

Does the dialogue work well (or not)?

Do the illustrations work well? Do they help you follow the story? Do they add to the atmosphere?

What did you especially like about the book (e.g. characters, action, dialogue, illustrations)?

What didn't you like about the book?

How did you feel while reading the story? For example, was it hard to put down or was it hard to keep reading? Did you care about what happened to the characters?

Who do you think the book is suitable for? What age? Boys or girls in particular? Readers who like a particular kind of book?

2 Now write your review below, using your notes.

Introduction ______________________________

Description (characters, setting, plot, illustrations) ______________________________

Judgment ______________________________

Chapter 9 Writing an information report

In an information report, your aim is to give your audience factual information on a topic. Many reports are about groups of things (e.g. sign languages), but some are about one particular thing (e.g. Morse Code).

STRUCTURE

LANGUAGE

Sign languages

What exactly are sign languages? One way to define them is to say they are methods of communication that do not involve words. Although we don't know for certain, human beings have probably been communicating with signs since the Stone Age—using hand and body signs or imitating the noises of animals and birds to communicate.

Ancient sign systems

Many indigenous cultures, such as the Aboriginal Australians and American Indians, used ancient sign language systems to communicate silently or across great distances. Maori dance is also a kind of sign language, with each movement standing for a particular word or thought, and each dance telling a story.

Body language

All cultures, however, use face, hand and body gestures to show others how they think and feel. This is called 'body language'. For example, English-speaking cultures show agreement by nodding their heads and disagreement by shaking their heads from side to side. However, body language is not the same in all cultures. In some cultures, the English speaker's sign for 'no' means 'yes'!

Finger alphabet and deaf languages

One special kind of sign language is the finger alphabet used by people who cannot hear. This consists of one sign for each letter of the alphabet —made using fingers, thumbs and hand movements. However, deaf people mostly use a sign language that has signs for complete words and complex thoughts. The language used by Australians and New Zealanders is called Auslan.

Using objects as signs

Communicating with flags, smoke, fire and drums are other kinds of sign systems. These systems were often first developed for use in wartime. Alexander the Great, for example, used trumpets, flags and torches to give orders in battle. Julius Caesar used horns and tubas to direct the foot soldiers and trumpets to command the cavalry. We still use these kinds of sign systems. Think of a trumpet used to announce an important person, a flag used to start a race or a flashing light used to indicate danger.

Humans are still inventing sign systems to meet their communication needs. The short cut 'smiley' symbols used in text messaging are just one example. Do you know what these symbols mean?

:-)   ;-)   :-o   :-(:'   :-|| (( )):**

Introduction to topic: often a definition

Information organised by sub-topics in paragraphs and under headings

Topic sentences used to help us understand main ideas

Factual information (not your opinions or personal experiences)

Conclusion (not always needed)

Mainly ***factual adjectives***

Topic word (sign language, signs) repeated to link ideas

Usually ***present tense of verbs*** (timeless present)

Technical words to talk about the topic

Explanations of terms readers might not understand

Often ***passive form of verb*** (e.g. *were developed*)

What did you read?

1. What are "sign languages"? ______________________________

____

2. True or false?

   a We know exactly how early humans communicated with each other. ________

   b Dance can be a kind of sign language. ________

   c Body language is used in all cultures. ________

   d Deaf people mainly use the finger alphabet to communicate. ________

   e Sign systems using objects like flags have been around for a very long time. ________

3. These sentences could be added at the end of some of the paragraphs of the report. Write the paragraph numbers below.
   a ___ Think of the Maori 'haka' dance performed by New Zealand footballers before international matches.
   b ___ It is possible that this is how real language began.
   c ___ There is now a dictionary of Auslan signs.
   d ___ So be warned! You need to be careful when travelling to other countries.

4. Why do you think deaf people use ***Auslan*** more than the finger alphabet? ______________

____

(And, by the way, can you work out where the word ***Auslan*** comes from?)

5. Why do you think musical instruments, flags and torches have been used to communicate in battle?

____

How was it written?

1. Circle the best answer. Why do you think the writer defined "sign languages"?
   a Because the reader might not have ever used sign language
   b Because no one knows what sign language is
   c Because the reader might not know exactly what sign language is

2. One way we link ideas in a report is to use the topic word or a similar word many times. Go through the text and underline these words: ***signs***, ***sign languages*** or ***sign systems***. How many times were they used? _____

3. To make the ideas clear to the reader, the writer used H __ __ __ __ __ __ S and P __ __ __ __ __ __ __ __ S.

4. The writer also uses T __ __ __ __ sentences to help us understand the main point of each paragraph. Underline these sentences in paragraphs 2, 3, 4 and 5.

5. The sentences below are on the topic of sign languages, but they would not be suitable in this report. Why?
   I know all the letters of the finger alphabet.
   Last night I tried using sign language instead of words at home but I only lasted five minutes.

____

Spelling and meaning

exactly	sign	language	methods	communication
certain	imitating	indigenous	cultures	ancient
systems	gestures	alphabet	announce	symbols

Tip for superior spellers
Breaking a word into **syllables** helps you avoid missing out letters in long words (e.g. comm-un-i-ca-tion, im-i-ta-ting). Don't worry too much about which way you break up the consonants. The important thing is to have one **vowel sound** in each syllable (e.g. s**y**m-b**o**ls).

1 Say the words in the word box out loud, breaking them into syllables (one vowel sound per syllable).

a Which word has only one syllable? ______________

b Which two words have three syllables? ______________ ______________

c Which two words have four syllables? ______________ ______________

d Which word has the most syllables? ______________

e How many syllables do most of the words have? ______ Give three examples.

______________ ______________ ______________

2 ***-ure*** at the ends of words (e.g. gest***ure***, cult***ure***) is a syllable that you do not hear very clearly. This makes it difficult to spell. Can you unscramble these ***-ure*** words?

a JINUER

____

b CPITRUE

____

c EASMURE

____

d SSPREUER

____

e RTAESURE

____

f SLEIREU

____

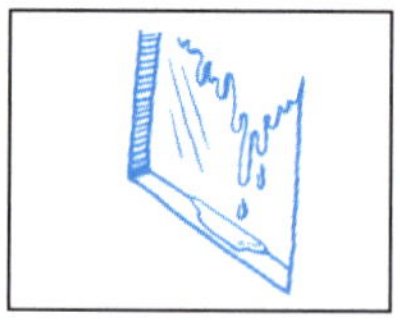

g OIMSTRUE

____

3 a Some of the words in the word box are synonyms (words with similar meanings). Can you write the three synonym pairs from the word box here?

S ______________ S ______________

M ______________ S ______________

L ______________ C ______________

b Which words in the word box are synonyms for these words?

i definite ______________________ ii precisely ______________________

iii native ______________________ iv copying ______________________

v societies ______________________ vi letters ______________________

vii very old ______________________ viii expressions ______________________

Grammar—Adjectival clauses

We often want to add extra detail to the noun or noun group. One way we can do this is by adding an adjectival clause. In these examples, the noun group is underlined and the adjectival clause is in **bold**.

Examples They are methods of communication **that do not involve words**.

Deaf people mostly use a sign language **that has signs for complete words and complex thoughts**.

Adjectival clauses usually begin with ***who***, ***which***, ***whose***, ***that*** or ***where***. They allow us to add quite complicated detail.

For adding simpler details to the noun we can use **adjectives** (e.g. **great** distances, **flashing** light, **important** person) or **adjectival phrases** (e.g. methods **of communication**, noises **of animals**).

Can you match the adjectival clauses on the right to the main clauses on the left so that they make sense? The nouns they add detail to are underlined.

- **a** Cryptologists are people
- **b** The science of breaking codes is cryptology
- **c** Ciphers are codes
- **d** Street signs and street lights are codes
- **e** A secret code is a code
- **f** Braille is a kind of code
- **g** Computers use a code
- **h** No one knew the secret place

- i that was developed to help the blind read.
- ii whose job is breaking secret codes.
- iii that everyone knows about.
- iv that are made by scrambling letters.
- v which means "secret word" in Greek.
- vi that translates everything into "on" or "off" terms.
- vii that only a few people know.
- viii where he had hidden the key.

Punctuation—Capital letters

You know that **capital letters** are used for **proper nouns** that are the names of people and places. However, you need to remember that they are also used for other proper nouns too (e.g. periods of time, wars and battles, brands, special methods or systems, titles, nationalities, languages and organisations).

1 Look back at the text on page 66 and underline all the words that have been capitalised. Think about why capitals were needed.

2 Can you put capitals where needed in these sentences? (Don't forget the ones at the start of the sentences.)

a a system of black and white smoke is used in st peter's square in rome to show if a new pope has been selected in the vatican.

b the international code of signals is a system of coloured flags standing for numbers and letters.

c the morse code system of dots and dashes was very important for communication in world war one.

d a young blind man called louis braille invented a brilliantly simple system to enable blind people to read with their fingers. it is called braille after its inventor.

Can you help?

In the paragraphs below the capital letters, commas and full stops have been left out. Read the paragraph through and add punctuation where needed. (Some full stops have been left in to help you.)

The Morse Code

the morse code was invented by samuel morse in 1837 morse had just invented a machine that could send electrical impulses over wires across great distances it was called the "electric telegraph". however the machine could not send words so morse had to invent a system of communication to make it useful. morse decided to base his system on short and long clicks the short clicks would be shown as dots in his code and the long clicks would be shown as dashes morse worked out which letters were used most in the english language and gave them the simplest click combinations morse code can be used anywhere as long as you have something that makes a sound. you can also send morse code using torches—short flashes for dots and long flashes for dashes

Puzzle time

Here is the whole Morse Code alphabet:

A •_	B _•••	C _•_•	D _••
E •	F ••_•	G __•	H ••••
I ••	J •___	K _•_	L •_••
M __	N _•	O ___	P •__•
Q __•_	R •_•	S •••	T _
U ••_	V •••_	W •__	X _••_
Y _•__	Y __••		

1 Which letters do you think are the three we use most frequently, based on what you just read about Morse's method above? ____ ____ ____

2 Can you translate these Morse Code messages?

••• ___ •••

___ •••_ • •_• •_ _• _•• ___ ••_ _

_•• •_ _• __• • •_•

3 Joke! The question in this joke is in ordinary writing but the answer is in Morse Code.
What goes dot dot croak dash dash croak?

__ ___ •_• ••• •   _ ___ •_ _••

4 Rebuses are picture puzzles. Can you work out what these rebus warnings mean?

Your turn to write

Tip for absolutely astonishing writers

In a report, you often have to use special technical words or expressions to write about your topic. It is very important to explain these words or expressions if you think your reader might not understand them.

1 Here is some information about a very special kind of sign language—the Braille system for people who are blind. Use the information in the box to draft a report on the topic in the space on the next page.

- Use your own words where possible.
- Leave out any information you do not understand.
- Change the order of the information if you think you need to.
- Keep to the facts and don't include your own opinions.
- Use some examples from the diagram.

The Braille system

- Braille—kind of sign language—a 'touch alphabet' developed to help the blind read
- Before Braille—many systems to help blind people—all using raised lettering
- Problem with early systems—blind could not learn to write them
- 1824—Louis Braille—invented very simple system—easy to read and to write
- Louis only 15 years old—blind since 3
- Knew about a system being developed to help French soldiers read important messages at night—this system too complicated
- System of dots on oblong block—block called the 'Braille cell'
- Raised dots on block—from one to six
- 63 combinations of dots possible—so whole alphabet and punctuation marks possible
- Helped millions of blind people enjoy reading and writing
- About 100 Braille newspapers and magazines

Here is the alphabet in Braille.

Braille alphabet

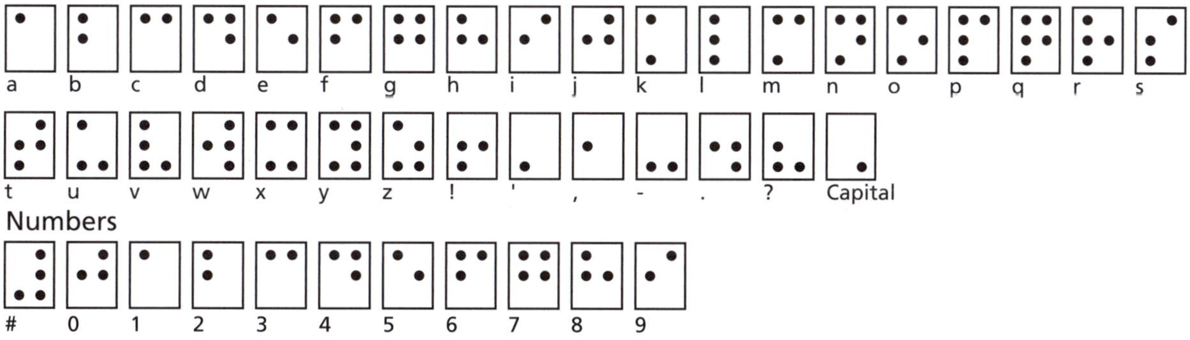

Introduction

History

Louis Braille's system

Examples (including diagrams)

Conclusion

2 You might want to do some research of your own about a kind of sign language and write a report in your Writer's Notebook. Here are some suggestions:

- The International Code of Signals (coloured flags)
- Semaphore
- American Indian Sign Language
- Australian Aboriginal Sign Language
- Auslan
- Picture languages
- Body language
- Secret codes and ciphers

Follow these steps to write your report.

- Do some research to find out some facts about your topic.
- Decide what you want to include in your report (you can't include everything).
- Organise your facts under three or four sub-topics.
- Begin your draft report with a definition of your topic.
- Draft your sub-topic paragraphs.
- Revise your draft and check your spelling, punctuation and grammar. Check too that you have kept your report factual and not included your own opinions.

DO YOU KNOW?

Do you know the complete finger alphabet? Here it is. See how quickly you can learn to use it.

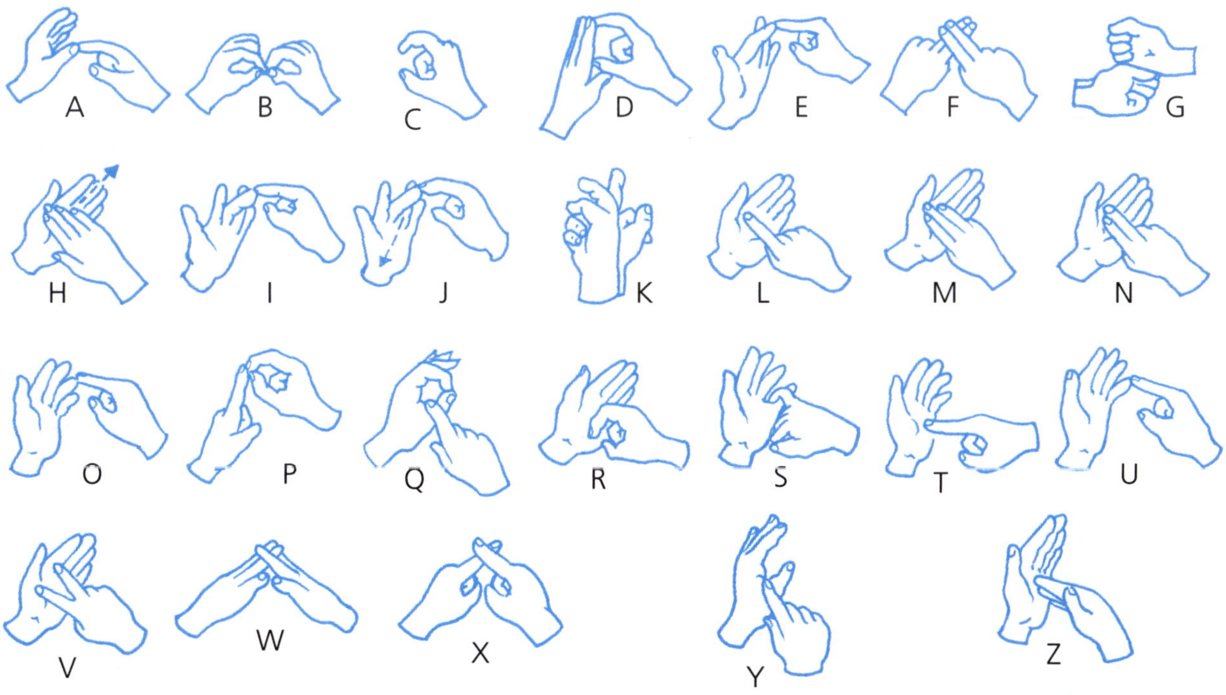

Chapter 10 Writing an exposition

The aim of an exposition is to give your opinion on a topic and to persuade your reader that your opinion is right. You often see expositions in newspapers and magazines where readers are asked to write in with their views, as in this example.

STRUCTURE | LANGUAGE

Have your say!

Each month in Have your Say! we ask you to tell us what you think on an important science and technology issue. This month's issue is: ***Should we be spending millions on the Search for Extraterrestrial Intelligence (SETI)?*** *We had a terrific response, with readers divided equally on the question. Have you made up your mind yet?*

Introduction to topic and statement of opinion

I definitely believe that we should be spending millions looking for extraterrestrials. I know some people think it is a waste of money because there are many things on our own planet we could spend the money on, but I do not think that this should stop our quest for knowledge. Here are my arguments.

Words to show the strength of your opinion (adverbs: *definitely*, *really*; and modals: *can*, *might*)

Thinking verbs

Arguments to support opinion organised in paragraphs

Firstly, if there is another kind of life form out there, we need to know about it. Imagine what would happen if aliens just suddenly arrived on Earth, and we were not prepared for them. It would be a disaster, even if they did not mean to hurt us. The film *E.T: The Extra-Terrestrial* shows how things could go wrong. The only way to be prepared for contact with aliens is to find them first.

Usually ***present tense***

Paragraphs begin with ***topic sentences*** which state arguments

Secondly, if we find life on another planet it might help the human species survive. For example, if Earth becomes impossible to live on because of global warming, the hole in the ozone layer or some other environmental problem, we might be able to go to that planet to live.

Connectives to link ideas

Thirdly, finding life on another planet might make humans behave better. It might make us be nicer to each other because we would see we were all part of the one species. We would also have to stop believing that the universe was ours, and that might make us take better care of our own planet.

Other sentences in paragraph develop arguments

Conclusion repeating opinion and perhaps a comment to round off

To sum up, I think we should spend as much money as we can on searching for extraterrestrials for the good of all humans. Besides, I think there must be something out there and I would really like to know what it is and where it is. Wouldn't you?

Kamal J., Queensland

What did you read?

1. Kamal thinks we should be searching for extraterrestrials. True or false? ________________

2. Which of these reasons does Kamal mention in support of his point of view? (Tick)
   - a We need to know about any extraterrestrials so we are prepared for contact. ___
   - b We should find aliens and destroy them, before they destroy us. ___
   - c We might be able to live on another planet if we are in trouble. ___
   - d It might make us behave better towards each other. ___
   - e It might make us take better care of our planet. ___
   - f It would give us lots more good material to make movies about. ___
   - g We must find out everything we can about everything. ___
   - h We need to control the universe. ___

3. Circle the best answer. Why does Kamal think we need to find aliens before they find us?
   - a To kill them
   - b To be prepared for them
   - c To show we are friendly

4. What two environmental problems might lead us to go and live on another planet, according to Kamal? ____

   ____

5. Kamal thinks finding aliens might make us behave better towards each other. Why?

   ____

How was it written?

1. Kamal tells us his opinion on the topic in the ___ ___ ___ ___ ___ sentence, so his readers will be absolutely C ___ ___ ___ ___ about his arguments.

2. Circle the best answer. Why does Kamal mention an argument against his point of view in the second sentence?
   - a To show he has thought about both sides
   - b To show how stupid the other argument is
   - c To show he is smart

3. Kamal gives three reasons to support his point of view. Why does he put each reason in a separate paragraph? ____

4. In paragraphs 2 and 3, Kamal uses an example to support his argument. Underline the sentence in each paragraph where he does this.

5. Kamal uses connectives to link up his ideas (e.g. ***firstly***, ***also***). Which connective does he use to show he is finishing off his argument? ________________

6. Circle the best answer. Kamal adds a personal comment at the end and a question to other readers. Why do you think he does this?
   - a To persuade them to agree with him
   - b To make them laugh
   - c To make his point of view clearer

7. Did you find Kamal's writing persuasive? Give your reasons.

   ____

Spelling and meaning

science	technology	issue	search	extraterrestrial
intelligence	question	definitely	quest	knowledge
arguments	aliens	impossible	ourselves	universe

1 Use words from the word box in these sentences and then learn all words using the **look–say–cover–write–check** method.

a An ______________________ is a being from somewhere outside Earth.

b It is ________________ to know everything about our ______________, but we should try.

c A ___________ is a kind of _______________ for an answer.

d I ___________________ believe we will find aliens one day.

e People will never agree on the _____________________ of SETI.

f You need to support your opinion with strong ______________________.

g The word "______________" means "a stranger" or "a foreigner" as well as a creature from another planet.

h If we find aliens they might not have _________________________ like ours, or

___________________ of the universe.

Many words in English begin with a **prefix**, which goes before a word or word base to make a new word (e.g. ***extra-*** in ***extraterrestrial*** and ***extraordinary***). Often these prefixes are from Latin. Knowing the meaning of prefixes helps us work out new words when we meet them.

2 a ***Super-***, ***sub-***, ***trans-*** and ***inter-*** are common prefixes. Look at the lists of words with these prefixes (below). Can you work out what each prefix means?

super = __________	**sub** = ____________	**trans** = __________	**inter** = __________
superman superhuman supermarket supernatural supernova	submarine submerge subterranean subtraction subway	transport transatlantic transform transfusion transmission	international intergalactic interaction interchange internet

b Which of the above words has the following meanings? Use your dictionary if needed.

i Sending a message from one place to another: ________________________

ii To place underneath the surface: ________________________

iii Beneath the earth: ________________________

iv A very bright kind of new star: ______________________

v Swapping places; road junction: ______________________

vi To do with the space between galaxies: ______________________

Grammar—Modals and adverbs

When we write opinion texts, we need to show how strongly we believe something or how sure we are about what we say.
One way we do this is by using **adverbs** such as ***definitely***, ***really***, ***perhaps***, ***maybe***, ***surely***, ***certainly***, ***possibly***, ***probably*** and ***likely***.
Examples I definitely believe that we should be spending millions …
I would really like to know …
Another way we do this is by using **modals** such as ***can***, ***might***, ***may***, ***could***, ***will***, ***should***, ***must***.
Examples … it might help the human species to survive.
We should spend as much money as we can …
Modals are part of the **verb group**. Often we use modals and adverbs together to show what we think.
Example We must definitely keep looking for aliens.

Look at the sentences below. For each group, write:

- 1 for the strongest, most certain opinion
- 3 for the weakest, least certain opinion
- 2 for the opinion in between

a We will certainly need to find another planet to live on. ___

We might need to find another planet to live on. ___

We will need to find another planet to live on. ___

b We should use the money for problems here on Earth. ___

We must use the money for problems here on Earth. ___

We could use the money for problems here on Earth. ___

c Finding aliens could teach us something about ourselves. ___

Finding aliens is sure to teach us something about ourselves. ___

Finding aliens might possibly teach us something about ourselves. ___

d We should definitely put money towards more space exploration. ___

Perhaps we should put money towards more space exploration. ___

We should probably put money towards more space exploration. ___

DID YOU KNOW?
People all over the world are helping to find extraterrestrials by using their home computers. The SETI@home project gives people a free screensaver and then gets to use their computer power to pick up strange radio signals from space. Imagine what it would be like to be the person to find an ET!

Punctuation—Abbreviations

We often use an **abbreviation** instead of a group of words for a well-known idea.
Usually we make the abbreviation by taking the first letter of each important word, but sometimes we add a letter from the middle of one of the words.
Example **SETI** for **S**earch for **E**xtra**t**errestrial **I**ntelligence
We don't put full stops between the letters in these kinds of abbreviations.
When we mention the idea the **first time**, we give the full form and put the abbreviation in brackets.
Example Search for Extraterrestrial Intelligence (SETI)

1 Can you fill in the missing letters to make these well-known groups of words? Write the abbreviation in capital letters.

a _ nidentified _ lying _ bject ______________

b _ nternational _ pace _tation ______________

c _ xtra _ ensory _ erception ______________

d _ ational _ eronautic and _ pace _ dministration ______________

2 Which abbreviation from activity 1 matches these ideas?

a What aliens might use to travel to Earth ______________

b The American organisation that might find aliens ______________

c The space vessel that might see aliens first ______________

d What aliens might use to think ______________

Can you help?

This student has written about SETI also, but her arguments are not as clear as Kamal's because she does not use words to link her ideas (connectives).
Can you write one of the connectives from the box below in her text where you see the spaces.

secondly	also	first of all	for example	as well as this

I feel that spending large amounts of money for SETI is a complete waste of money. ______________ there are many problems on our own planet. ______________ there are millions of people in developing countries who are starving. ______________ there are children in our own cities who are homeless and on drugs. ______________ there are farmers who are always struggling because of drought. ______________ we won't find any life on other planets. I think we would have heard from someone already if they were out there.

Puzzle time

1 ***Extraterrestrial*** is a very long word. How many words can you make from its letters? (There are at leas twenty.)

______________ ______________ ______________ ______________

______________ ______________ ______________ ______________

______________ ______________ ______________ ______________

______________ ______________ ______________ ______________

______________ ______________ ______________ ______________

______________ ______________ ______________ ______________

2 Fill in the missing letters using the clues. Then read the first letters of each word to get another word meaning a person who travels in space.

1. ___ ___ I ___ ___ (A stranger from another planet)
2. ___ ___ G ___ ___ ___ ___ (Scientists are looking for radio ______ from intelligent life in outer space.)
3. ___ ___ K ___ - ___ ___ ___ (When a rocket leaves Earth)
4. ___ ___ C ___ ___ ___ (Another name for a space ship)
5. ___ ___ B ___ ___ (To revolve around a planet)
6. ___ ___ P ___ ___ ___ ___ (It seems unlikely that there would be any life on this large planet)
7. ___ ___ R (There's none of this in space)
8. ___ ___ O (Spacecraft of alien life forms—abbreviation)
9. ___ ___ R ___ ___ ___ ___ ___ ___ ___ L (A creature from our own planet Earth)

A person who travels in space is an ______________________

Your turn to write

Tip for terrific terrestrial writers

Your opinion will be far more convincing if you have some facts to support it, so you might need to do some research before you start writing. Sometimes, however, you will have to depend more on your logic—clear thinking—to support your view.

1 There are always two (or more) ways to look at an issue, and it is good to prepare for writing by thinking about them all.

a Here are some arguments for and against searching for extraterrestrials. In the spaces, jot down one idea or example to develop each argument.

For	Against
1. We must always search for knowledge …	1. There are many problems on Earth to sort out first …
2. Finding ETs is the most exciting thing imaginable …	2. Aliens might destroy us if we find them or we might destroy them …

3. There must be other creatures out there …	3. We are unlikely to find anything …
4. We might need to live on another planet …	4. It would not benefit us here on Earth …
5. We might learn something from aliens …	

b Now decide the side you most believe in, and choose **two** arguments only to write about below.

Topic and your opinion

Your first argument

Your second argument

Conclusion: repeat your opinion and sum up

2 Now choose one of these other space topics from the "Have your say!" column and write your opinion. Use your own paper or your Writer's Notebook.

Topics
- If we find extraterrestrials, should we make contact with them?
- Is space research of any kind worth the money?
- Should we try to establish a colony on the Moon?

Remember:
- Introduce the topic and your opinion.
- Use logical arguments and facts to support your opinion.
- Organise your main arguments in paragraphs.
- Use connectives to link your ideas (e.g. firstly, secondly, for example).
- Use modals (e.g. can, might) and adverbs (e.g. definitely) to show how strong your opinion is.
- Write a conclusion to sum up your arguments.
- Proofread your writing for spelling, punctuation and grammar.

Answers on pages 99–100

Chapter 11 Writing for school research projects

This chapter will help you with school projects. It is organised differently from the other chapters in the book. It has three sections:

- Finding information
- Using your own words
- Writing a bibliography

You will see how one student worked on a Year 5 project on the topic of "Ancient Civilisations", and you will do some work on this topic too.

The project task

The project task was to research and write about:

- **a city** built by an ancient civilisation:
  - the location of the city
  - the purpose of the city
  - the structure and layout of the city
- **everyday life** in the region, for example, family life, food and shopping, leisure time activities and education.

The student in this example chose to focus on Ancient Greece.

Tips for premier project writers

- Don't just copy all the information you find into your project. Select information and then put it into your own words to show you understand what you are writing about.
- Don't use information you don't understand. Either leave it out altogether or ask an adult to explain it.
- Keep your mind on what you have been asked to do: the project topic and project task. Ignore everything else.
- Make sure you say where you got your information from (e.g. a book, a newspaper article, a website).

Finding information

Let's look at what the student did to choose an **ancient Greek city** to write about and to find information on that city.

First, the student looked in the contents page of a book called *The Ancient Greeks* for chapters that:

- mentioned cities he had heard of
- contained words which could be names of cities
- mentioned city life.

The ticks show the chapters he decided to look up. Would you have chosen the same chapters?

CONTENTS

Then, he looked at the chapters to see what information they had, and decided to write about Mycenae. The chapter on "Mycenae and the Mycenaeans" had plenty of information that looked interesting and easy to understand.

You will see this student's writing about Mycenae on page 85.

1 Now let's see what information you can find for the second part of the project: **everyday life**.

a Look again at the Contents page of *The Ancient Greeks* above. Tick the chapters that might have some useful information on the topic of everyday life. Tick the chapters that are *definitely* on the topic *and* those that *might* be on the topic.

b Which chapter do you think might have the most information about **everyday life**? ____________

____

2 Did you notice that the Contents page includes an index? You should always look up the index as well as the Contents pages of books, but often you have to think up words to look for. Write down two or three words you might use to look up an index for the topic **Everyday life**.

____

____

Using your own words

Here is the information about Mycenae from the book *The Ancient Greeks*.
Look at the next page to see how our student selected from this information and changed the words to make his own text. You don't have to read this text in detail—look mainly at the parts marked with lines from the next page.

Mycenae and the Mycenaeans

The Mycenaean people

The Mycenaeans (also called Achaeans) dominated Greece after the Minoan civilisation on Crete collapsed. The Mycenaean period lasted from approximately 1600 to 1100 BC. Much of the information we have about this very powerful civilisation has come from the objects, weapons and armour they put in the royal graves in their city kingdoms.

The Mycenaeans were a very warlike people who established fortified city kingdoms all over the Peloponnese, the large southern Greek peninsula. They were not united politically, but they were linked by their culture and religious beliefs. They also spoke the same form of the Greek language and shared a common way of life. They were adventurous, daring master seafarers, building up a profitable trade over the entire eastern Mediterranean.

Mycenae

Mycenae was the greatest and most important of the Mycenaean cities. Mycenae is remembered in poetry and legend as "rich in gold". It was located 10 kilometres north of Argos and 90 kilometres south-west of Athens in the Peloponnese.

The Mycenae acropolis

Like all Mycenaean cities, Mycenae was a fortified city called an 'acropolis'. This means "high city" in Greek. It was designed as a military stronghold—a walled fortress with high walls all around it to make it invulnerable to attack and relatively easy to defend. The walls were extremely thick (up to seven metres) and very strong. The walls were made of huge blocks of stone so big that they were thought in later times to be the work of the mythical one-eyed giants known as the Cyclopes.

City layout

The main gateway to the city was the Lion Gate. This was decorated with sculptures of two lions, which are thought to be the symbols of the Mycenaean royal family.

Along the inside wall of the city were the houses of artists, craftsmen and other city workers. These were the areas that were most vulnerable to attack. In the centre of the city furthest from the walls and possible destruction was the royal palace. The palace was not just a royal residence. It was a military headquarters, administrative centre and a workplace for many skilled craftsmen. It was also the place where all the agricultural produce from the surrounding countryside was kept until use or export. Craft and imports were also stored in the palace rooms.

WHAT THE STUDENT DID

Wrote a sentence to introduce the topic

Used headings from the project task

Changed order of information to suit the project task

Left out information not directly on the topic or task

Summarised

Gave meanings of words he thought he needed to explain (e.g. ***fortified***)

Used own words as much as possible

Gave the author of the book used and the date—full details will be in the bibliography

Linked writing to pictures used on another page of the project

Yesterday's city: Mycenae

Mycenae was the most important city on mainland Greece from about 1600 to 1100 BC, and the greatest city of the Mycenaean people who dominated Greece at this time. The Mycenaeans were an adventurous, warlike people who shared the same culture, language and religious beliefs.

Location

Mycenae was located 90 kilometres south-west of Athens in the Peloponnese, the large southern Greek peninsula. (See map below.)

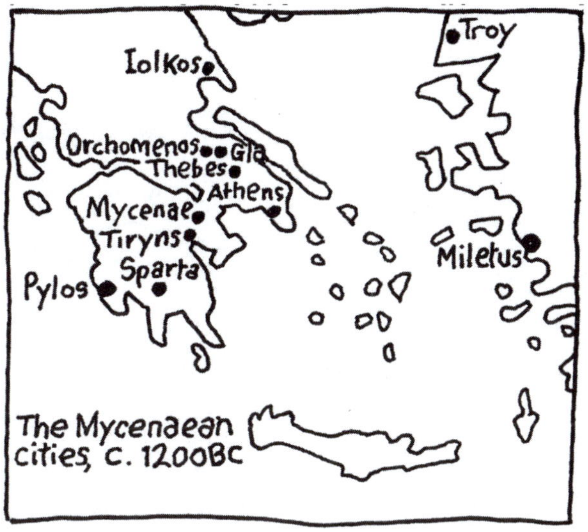

Purpose

Mycenae was built as a military stronghold. It was a fortified city. This means it was built in a way so it could be defended from attack. It was also an 'acropolis' which means "high city" in Greek. It was designed as a walled fortress with high walls all around it to make it easier to defend. Some parts of the wall were seven metres thick. The blocks of stone were so big that later people thought they had been placed there by the Cyclopes, mythical one-eyed giants!

Structure and layout

The city was entered via the Lion Gate—a large archway decorated with two lions. Along the inside wall of the city were the houses of artists, craftsmen and other city workers. In the centre of the city furthest from the walls and risk of destruction was the royal palace. The palace was more than a royal residence. It was the headquarters for the military and the centre of administration. It was also the workplace for the skilled craftsmen of the city. It was also the place where all the agricultural products from the surrounding countryside were kept until they were used or exported.
(Gilhooley, 1995)

The map of the city on the next page shows the layout.

1 Read this text about one aspect of **everyday life** in ancient Greece. Then complete the shorter version below using the information and your own words. (Notice that the focus has shifted from the market place to how the people spent their days.)

The agora

The social and commercial centre of every Greek city was the 'agora', or market place. A typical agora was surrounded by a U- or L-shaped building called a 'stoa'. This was the building that held the shops. The shop areas were usually protected from the sun by a long shady verandah area supported by columns.

The open-air area near the stoa was set up with stalls just like in a modern day street market. Farmers would come to sell their produce at the stalls—fruit and vegetables, cheese, eggs and meat. Craftsmen usually lived close to the agora and displayed their wares from their home workshops.

Women did most of the shopping for the household, though often it was female servants rather than the mistress of the house.

It was not only women who went to the agora. Men went there to look for work, to change or borrow money, to look for slaves for their households or just to chat with their friends in the shade of the stoa colonnades.

Shopping

A typical day for a Greek man or woman began with a trip to the ____________________ or ____________________. A woman—either the ____________________ or a ____________________ of the household—might first walk around the shops in the ____________________, which was ____________________. Then she might look at the ____________________ brought in fresh from the countryside by ____________________. She might also look in the ____________________ ____________________ where the craftsmen sold ____________________. A man might spend most time ____________________, ____________________ or ____________________. Or he might just relax and ____________________.

2 Now read this text on another aspect of **everyday life** in ancient Greece and write your version below. Begin with the sentence provided. As with activity 1, focus more on people and how they spent their time.

Remember:

- Change the order of the information.
- Use your own words where you can.
- Explain words if needed.
- Use some examples only—not all.

Education

The aim of education in ancient Greece was to produce a good citizen who could participate fully in running the state or city. Another important aim was physical fitness.

Education was not free so it was really only the children of richer families who went to school for very long. Girls did not go at all. They were educated at home by their mothers.

Boys who were well educated received training in reading, writing and arithmetic, in music and poetry, and in dancing and athletics. These lessons took place at three different kinds of schools.

Their education began at 7 years of age and went on until they started their military training at 18 years.

Many families employed a slave to supervise their son's learning. This slave, called a 'paidogogos' walked the boy to school and waited there while the boy had his lessons so that he could be sure he listened and behaved well.

Boys from more wealthy homes spent their day at school. They ____________________

Writing a bibliography

It is very important to say where you got your information from—which book, which website, which newspaper article and so on. This is called **referencing**.

The most important part of referencing for you is the **bibliography**.

If you can, you should also say where you got your information from **on the page you use it**. Look back at page 85 to see how the student gave the author's surname and date of the book he used. He wrote (***Gilhooley, 1995***). You can see in the box below how he gave the full details of the book in his Bibliography.

Here is the student's full Bibliography. Look at it and read the notes at the side.

Website	Athens Museum, *Cities of Ancient Greece* (website) www.athens.com/cities. Last updated 2002
Book	Gilhooley, M., 1995 , *The Ancient Greeks*. Brown Publishing Company, Sydney
Book	Jones, J. and King, L., 2001, *Ancient Civilisations: Greece*. Hector Publishing. Melbourne
Newspaper article	Luscombe, R., "Travel back in time: touring in Greece", *Eastern Courier*, 23/4/04
Website	Young, B., *Mycenae* (website) www.caldo.com/Mycenae, no date

- List in alphabetical order by author's name
- Put organisation if no person given as author
- Give the date of publication
- Give a website date if you can see one
- Put titles in *italics* if typing ("quotation marks" if handwriting)

Follow the models above to write these materials as a bibliography. Remember to put them in alphabetical order.

A book called Athens by Jane Brooks, published in 1999 in London by Tuttle Publishers
A website called Greek Mythology, by Martins University, www.myths.martins.edu.au
A newspaper article headed Greek Treasures by Kenneth Tagg, which appeared in the Northern News on the 3rd February 2004
A book called Life in Ancient Greece by Anthony Nolan, published in 2000 in New York by Jansens

Your turn to write

You might be doing a research project at school right now. If so, keep this chapter close by to help you. If you are not working on a project, choose any topic you like to research and write up. Perhaps you could research and write about an ancient civilisation you are interested in.

DID YOU KNOW?

The Ancient Greeks were the first civilisation to discover many things we now take for granted. For example, in the 6th century BC, the Greek mathematician Pythagoras stated that the earth was round, but few believed him. The world did not accept this as truth until much, much later.

Answers on page 100

Answers

Chapter 1 — Pages 2–9

What did you read?

1 Because there were three activities
2 c
3 b
4 Josh pushed her out of the way to catch the ball; then, Josh did not even catch it.
5 She got two home runs.
6 The boys

How was it written?

1 What? Sport and Healthy Lifestyles Week; Who? Tara's school; Where? Recount does not say exactly; When? Last week
2 **a** After recess; **b** After lunch; **c** After bowling
3 How people in India do the 'salute to the sun' each morning
4 PAST
5 b
6 a

Spelling and meanings

2 tries, ponies, parties, libraries, territories, boundaries
3 **a** aerobics; **b** gymnastics; **c** athletics; **d** cricket; **e** rugby league; **f** hockey
4 **a** taekwondo; **b** bocce; **c** tai chi; **d** yoga

Grammar

1 On Wednesday, (we) walked to the Birraway Art Gallery, about two kilometres away. (We) looked at the paintings and sculptures. Some of the sculptures were absolutely huge. Afterwards, (we) had a lesson in cartooning with a cartoonist called Nick. (He) taught (us) some cool tricks to do when drawing figures, for example, how to show a person is moving. My cartoon was not the best (Kyle's and Tanama's were best as usual), but (it) was much better than the cartoons (I) usually do.

2 Possible answers:
a the girls; **b** The teacher;
c Henna; **d** Joe's cart OR My cart;
e Lina OR Josie

Punctuation

a Jenna does gymnastics and likes the parallel bars**,** the vault and the mat the best.
b Marko does three winter sports—soccer**,** ice hockey and gymnastics.
c Our teacher told us to bring sports shoes**,** a hat**,** sunscreen**,** a jacket and lunch money.
d We do exercises before school on Monday**,** Tuesday**,** Wednesday and Friday.
e In our last three matches we won**,** drew and lost.
f Forehands**,** backhands and volleys are all types of tennis strokes.

Can you help?

In Sport and Healthy Lifestyles Week, the first thing we did was yoga with Mrs Rowe and Mrs Godleman. It could put you to sleep! Then we did softball with Craig and Andrew. The helmets were the best. Then we played cricket with David Stanford. It was so much fun! The next day we did netball and tai chi. Tai chi was borrring! Wednesday was the teachers' strike (YES!) so nobody went to school. On Thursday we did the obstacle course. That was definitely the highlight of the week. After the break we did the beep test. I got 5.5. Afterwards we did rugby league. The next day we had to get to school early so we could go to tennis. It was really good fun. Later we did Coach Approach—there were five activities and handball was the best. In conclusion it was the best school week ever!

Puzzle time

1 ARCHERY, MATCH, COURT, SKIING, DIVING, YACHTING, GOALPOST, SHOTPUT, CAPTAIN, REFEREE, RACQUET, UMPIRE
2 HEALTHY

Your turn to write

1 a yes
  b no
  c When the boy kept swimming after a false start. Because it is funny and interesting—probably the part of the day that most students talked about afterwards

Chapter 2 Pages 10–17

What did you read?

1 a True; b False; c False; d False
2 c
3 a Probably not. The text says it was at dawn and that no one was awake. The boys probably would not have told them about their plans in case they were stopped.
  b Probably the younger brother. He annoys his brother, wouldn't sit still and was very scared. All these things make it sound like he is younger than his brother.
  c Probably yes. The narrator says they had been friends 'for that moment' so it sounds like he knows they will fight again.
4 a The relationship between the two brothers;
  b Possible other titles: "Brotherly Love" or "Boat Brothers"

How was it written?

1 a supposed to be;
  b As usual the only snag was my brother.
2 b. The dialogue is meant to show how they typically argue. It does not matter who says what—they always call each other names and argue like this.
3 It was really scary; frantically; I felt sick and dizzy; we were both exhausted; I have never been so embarrassed in my entire life; release from absolute panic; roaring with laughter
4 a shrouded; b stir; c snag; d oaf
5 a

Spelling and meaning

1 a exhausted; b invisible; c steer;
  d disappeared; e surroundings;
  f embarrassed; g clumsy; h totally;
  i realised
2 a chirrup, buzz; b rumbled, boomed;
  c whispered, whistled; d gurgled;
  e trill, chirrup, chatter; f rumbled, rattled;
  g thud, crash

Grammar

1 a [My brother and I] <u>were sitting</u> in an old canoe at dawn on the first morning of our holiday.
  b [No one else] <u>would be</u> awake for hours.
  c [The lake around us] <u>was</u> still and shrouded in mist.
  d [Water birds] <u>were starting</u> to stir.
  e [An invisible frog] <u>was croaking</u> in a nearby clump of rushes.
  f Once again [he] <u>started being</u> a total pain.
  g [We] <u>were</u> lost like helpless little children in a big city.
2 a Shortly afterwards Mr Stanovski turned the corner.
  b Ten small boys lined up at the counter.
  c I simply could not steer the bike.
  d Sanjay stayed completely silent.
  e The kookaburra laughed at us from the treetops.

Punctuation

a "Let me go!" she screamed.
b "Why can't I come with you now?" she asked.
c "Sit still," he shouted, "or the boat will go over."
d "I will show them," I whispered to myself.
e "I don't know where he is now," she cried softly.
f "You'll be very sorry," she said, "because I won't forget this quickly."
g Then I heard her say "Come over here. I'm under the dinner table."
h Josie asked "When will I be able to go home?"

Can you help?

It was an ordinary morning at Emerald Beach. Tamsin and I lazily made our way along the sand, planning how we would spend our precious last day of the summer holidays. It was a perfect day, except for a few greyish clouds a long way off on the horizon. Mm, maybe some rain later but for now the day was crystal clear. Some little children were playing happily near the water's edge, a fisherman was waiting patiently for the fish to bite, and in the distance some older boys and girls seemed to be having trouble launching a small speedboat.

Puzzle time

STAMMER, SPUTTER, MUMBLE, CHATTER, COMMENT, COMPLAIN, SNIFFLE, PROMISE, MUTTER, ANNOUNCE, DECLARE, MURMUR

Chapter 3 — Pages 18–25

What did you read?

1 **a** Orange juice (or other juice);
  b The child narrator
2 a
3 a
4 c
5 holes (where a child has pulled and poked at the bear's eyes)
6 put up with, or stand

How were they written?

1 **a** lurk; **b** lunge
2 blisters on the brain
3 **a** Eye gouges;
  b Bumps, / thumps and / Falls;
  c Nibbled on
4 **a** Are you feeling flat?
  b We will soon fix that!
5 The short, fast lines make you read the poem fast. This reflects how you put hair gel on quickly and you get a quick result.

Spelling and meaning

1 **a** daily; **b** notice; **c** cuddled; **d** career; **e** dribbled; **f** gouges; **g** slick; **h** excuses; **i** people; **j** bounced
2 **squeeze:** breeze, sneeze, please; **gel:** yell, bell, tell; **excuse:** goose, moose, Bruce; **dribble:** nibble, quibble, scribble
3 **a** wait in ambush; **b** prowl; **c** loiter; **d** linger; **e** cool their heels

Grammar

1 Possible answers:
  a Over the bridge and past the cave
  b Tiring, lazy days
  c Teacher glaring
  d Spinning fast on my skates
  e Children squealing
  f Rooms dark and cold
  g Woolly socks and long underwear

Punctuation

Most likely answers:
1 **a** Fast; **b** smooth and flowing
2 **a** Fast; **b** snappy

Puzzle time

As I was going up the stair
I met a man who wasn't there
He wasn't there again today
Oh, how I wish he'd go away.

Order in the court
The judge is eating beans
His wife is in the bathtub
Shooting submarines

Through the teeth
And past the gums
Look out stomach
Here it comes!

Chapter 4 — Pages 26–33

What did you read?

1 **a** cushion of air
2 **a** False; **b** False; **c** True; **d** False
3 Blow up a balloon: 2, Use glue: 1, Stretch the balloon neck: 3
4 The balloon hovercraft works because the air from the balloon forms a cushion between the CD and the surface.

How was it written?

1 The list of things you will need, because if you don't have these things you would not be able to follow the procedure.
2 glue, wait, blow up, twist, stretch, make sure, put, let go, try
3 a
4 No. You have to follow the steps in this order or the hovercraft would not stick together or move properly.

5 a If it is not firmly attached, it would probably fall apart once it moved.

b If it is not flat and smooth, the hovercraft would just stop at the first little bump. A real hovercraft could manage on a bumpy surface—as hovercrafts do on rough seas—but this hovercraft is not as strong as a real one.

6 b You might have said that diagrams of each step would have helped you. Diagrams are usually a great help in procedures.

Spelling and meaning

1 1. attached; 2. cardboard; 3. carefully; 4. couple; 5. cushion; 6. escaping; 7. exactly; 8. glide; 9. hovercraft; 10. literally; 11. middle; 12. moving; 13. surface; 14. thread; 15. usually

2 a Make sure the coloured side is facing upwards.

b Stick the wires in, making sure their ends are not touching.

c Keep squeezing the cloth until there is no more liquid left.

d Check the arrangement of the cards to be sure they are equally spaced.

e Draw lines on the paper, dividing it into twelve equal sections.

f Use staples or glue to stop the pages separating at the sides.

g Make different pictures by changing the pieces around.

h A knife with a serrated edge would be most useful.

3 Surfboard, fingerprint, greenhouse, waterproof, underwear, footprint, windmill, wetsuit, snowflake, tablespoon, crossword, aircraft, underwater, sunscreen, windsurf, spaceship (you might have some more)

Grammar

a Slice the bread finely to make sandwiches that are easy to eat.

b Cut the sandwiches diagonally so that they look attractive on the plate.

c Heat the frying pan and rub it lightly with butter.

d Divide the mixture evenly into four portions.

e Add all the ingredients and mix them together well.

f Spread the cheese mixture thickly on the bread.

g Leave overnight in a warm place.

Punctuation

Possible answer:

1. Use one ball only, and throw it from one hand to the other. Instead of looking at your two hands, as you normally would when you throw a ball, look at the highest point that the ball reaches. Practise until you feel very comfortable doing this.
2. Using two balls now, put one ball in each hand and throw ball 1 from one hand to the other. When ball 1 reaches its highest point, throw ball 2. Do not swap ball 2 from one hand to the other, but throw it as shown in the drawing. Practise this until you feel comfortable.
3. Using three balls now, do the same as you did in step 2, but this time take two balls in one hand and one ball in the other. Start throwing from the hand with the two balls. Throwing and catching is now a continuous activity. Try to force yourself to throw the balls backwards, because otherwise you will throw them forwards and drop them.

Can you help?

You will need:
Talcum powder
A saucer
A paintbrush
A magnifying glass

Puzzle time

GONDOLA, CHAIR LIFT, TROLLEY BUS, CATAMARAN, FUNICULAR

Chapter 5 Pages 34–41

What did you read?

1 To ask him to write another book in the series The Wind on Fire.

2 Adam's favourite book is *Slaves of Mastery*.

3 Most likely answer is fantasy. Adam mentions the Singer people and the Morah and these

are not known in our real world. He also imagines that Kestrel could come back to life.

4 c

5 It sounds like Kestrel dies, and the adventure ends for the characters mentioned—perhaps because of the Morah.

How was it written?

1 a paragraph 2; b paragraph 3; c paragraph 4; d paragraph 1

2 To be polite. It is nice to say something positive to a person before asking them for something. Also because his request does not make sense without understanding how much Adam loves the books.

3 a I was wondering if you would consider

b Would you write another book? 2; Can you write another book? 3; Would you please write another book? 1

4 He mentions how he could not stop reading the second book, AND he begged his mother to get him the third book.

5 You might say that William Nicholson would reply because the letter is interesting, OR because Adam makes it clear that he is a big fan, OR that he makes it very clear why he is writing, OR that he writes *PLEASE write a fourth book!* at the end.

Spelling and meaning

1 a actually; b equally; c finally; d annually; e generally/usually

2 I thought the book was the best adventure I had ever read, because the characters were so lively and interesting. I know there would be some problems in writing more books about the same characters, but one solution would be to invent some new ones. I would especially like to see Tristan find a new friend to take the place of Joseph. I am not very good at writing so I was wondering if you could give me some tips when you write back.

3 **Group:** tense, suspenseful, frightening, mysterious; **Group:** amusing, hilarious, comical, funny, humorous; **Group:** moving, sad, tragic, upsetting

Grammar

b Could you send me a free copy?

c May I make a suggestion?

d We would all love you to visit our school.

e Your readers would want you to keep writing.

f You could print more copies of the magazine.

g Could you please consider my request?

Punctuation

1 a The funniest poem I have heard is a Steven Herrick poem called "Science".

b I preferred "Blabber Mouth" to "Worry Warts" but "Two Weeks with the Queen" was my favourite.

c I've read four of Paul Jennings's books: "Unreal", "Unbelievable", "Uncanny" and "Unbearable".

d At our school we have a poetry competition and last year I recited "The Thong".

e I read an extract of "The Redback Leftovers" by Debra Oswald in "The Gazette".

f I watched "Around the Twist" on television every week when it was on.

2 parade, court, avenue, street, road, lane, drive, crescent

3 a Flat 2, 90 Valley Way
Springfield NSW 2777

b 356 Brighton Pde
Brighton QLD 4017

c 2/6 Fletcher St
Brooklyn TAS 7320

d 623 Berry Rd
Blackburn VIC 3130

e Flat 33, 23 Mill Ave
Fern Bay WA 2295

f 16 Bruce Cr
Dickson ACT 2602

Can you help?

a 3; b 2; c 4; d 7; e 1; f 6; g 5

Puzzle time

1 *Wind in the Willows* Kenneth Grahame; *Oliver Twist* Charles Dickens; *Matilda* Roald Dahl; *Boss of the Pool* Robin Klein; *Misery Guts* Morris Gleitzman; *Animalia* Graeme Base; *The Silver Sword* Ian Serralier; *The Magic Pudding*

Norman Lindsay

2 *Alice's Adventures in Wonderland*; *The Lion, the Witch and the Wardrobe*; *The Wizard of Oz*; *George's Marvellous Medicine*; *Fantastic Mr Fox*; *Peter Pan and Wendy*

Chapter 6 Pages 42–49

What did you read?

1 They begin life looking like fish and living in water, and then they become adults and live on land.
2 Inside the egg
3 Lungs replace its gills
4 c
5 It survives drought by making itself a water-filled jacket.
6 They warn predators of danger.

How was it written?

1 To capture the audience's interest
2 a
3 But actually frogs are quite remarkable, and that is why I want to tell you about them today. / One of the most interesting things about frogs is their life cycles. / One interesting example is the Australian water-holding frog … / So you see—frogs are not uninteresting, ugly … / They are some of the most fascinating, colourful creatures on earth.
4 Why is it, do you think, that frogs turn up in so many fairy tales and are hated and feared by beautiful princesses? / So firstly, what are frogs? / But did you know this is really singing?
5 a grapefruit
6 diet—paragraph 4, mating habits—paragraph 5, poisonous frogs—paragraph 7, life cycle—paragraph 3, different species—paragraph 6
7 So you see.

Spelling and meaning

3 dangerous, graceful, powerful, colourful, greenish, interesting, deadly, lively, astonishing
4 **a** cannibals; **b** amphibians; **c** emerges; **d** poisonous; **e** creatures; **f** gradually

Grammar

1 c/but: Tadpoles feed mainly on algae but they will sometimes tackle an insect swimming in the water.
2 a/and: The male toad protects the eggs from predators and (he) keeps them at the correct temperature until ready to hatch.
3 f/but: The frill-necked lizard usually keeps its frill folded flat, but it will raise it during courtship or when threatened.
4 d/and: The frill-necked lizard is exceptionally fast moving on the ground, and (it) mostly runs upright on its hind legs.
5 e/but: Green turtles used to be common in warm oceans, but today their numbers are a fraction of what they once were.
6 b/but: The green turtle is most at home underwater, but it must come to the surface every now and then to breathe air.

Punctuation

Possible answer: Frogs eat <u>any</u> animal that moves and is small enough to fit in their mouths—<u>even</u> snakes. And <u>here</u> is something not so nice about frogs. They are <u>cannibals</u>. They eat other frogs, <u>even</u> frogs of their own kind.
You've probably all heard frogs croaking in the garden. But did you know this is really <u>singing</u>? The male frog sings to attract females at breeding time. The female can recognise a male of her kind. She follows his song and finds him in the dark. <u>Very</u> romantic!

Can you help?

Possible answers:

1 1. Did you know that there are only 200 Siberian tigers left in the wild? 3. Siberian tigers are very beautiful and very rare. 2. The Siberian tiger is the largest cat in the whole world.
2 3. The orang-utan is the second largest primate. 1. In the Malay language, "orang" means "man" and "utan" means "jungle", so "orang-utan" means "man of the jungle". 2. The orang-utan is only found in Sumatra and Borneo.
3 3. The common clownfish lives on Australia's Great Barrier Reef. 1. Did you see the movie *Finding Nemo?* 2. The clownfish gets its name

from its white bands that look like circus face paint.

Puzzle time

a DEER; b WOLF; c MOOSE; d HORSE; e TIGER; f SHARK; g WHALE; h CAMEL

Chapter 7 Pages 50–57

What did you read?

1 flesh-eating, insects
2 a
3 nectar
4 the pressure of the insect. No, it won't close if the pressure is not great enough (that is, the insect is too small and light).
5 It drowns.
6 Because then it stays long enough to taste the nectar and falls in.

How was it written?

1 first
2 Bradley
3 a large seashell. To help us know what it looks like.
4 Bradley identifies the 'trap', the large spiky 'teeth', the bright colours and the beautiful scent.
5 **Venus Flytrap:** Insects attracted by nectar and colour. Insects land on trap. Trap closes. Insects digested. **Pitcher of Death:** Insects attracted by nectar. Insects slip on smooth surface. Insects forced down by slippery hairs. Insects fall into digestive fluid and drown. Insects digested.

Spelling and meaning

1 a vibrant; b nutrients; c hostile; d digest; e scent; f chamber; g pitcher; h fluid
2 a preying; b slipperiness; c beautiful; d extraordinarily; e easily; f hurried; g spikiness; h carrying; i annoying; j enjoyed
3 a nutrition; b digestion; c insecticide; d hostility; e fluidity; f vibrancy
4 a AMAZING; b FASCINATING; c INCREDIBLE; d UNBELIEVABLE; e ASTONISHING; f REMARKABLE

Grammar

1 a Insects are attracted to it because of the vibrant colours and sweet-scented nectar.
b Once the trap has swallowed an insect, it takes ten days to digest it.
c As you can probably tell by its name, it kills and eats insects.
d To catch flies and other insects, this plant needs a bait and a trap.
2 a v. People don't often keep this plant in the house, because it can be deadly.
b iv. You should really watch your step if you live in Malaysia!
c i. The fly gets stuck when it lands.
d ii. The plant eats the flies and insects, because it doesn't get nitrogen from the soil.
e iii. Venus Flytraps sometimes catch and eat small frogs, although they are not designed for large prey.
3 a I; b D; c I; d D; e I; f D

Punctuation

a Its; b it's; c its; d its; e It's

Can you help?

The Great Barrier Reef is the largest living structure on earth and is even visible from space. Most people know this reef is made of coral, but many people do not know how coral reefs form. Coral reefs look like rocks but they are actually animals. The reefs are made up of colonies of tiny creatures called polyps. These polyps produce limestone from their outer cells. The limestone gradually builds up around them, making them larger and larger. Every year as the polyps reproduce and new polyps grow, the reef expands. Each polyp is connected to its neighbours by strands of living tissues and this is how the polyps make up a whole reef.

Puzzle time

a MOSS; b FERN; c ALGAE; d FUNGUS

Chapter 8 Pages 58–65

What did you read?

1 families, friendship and forgiveness
2 verse

3 a Tom does not like: (any of these answers) the wall around Pacific Palms, how you have to use a PIN number to get into it, his father's obsession with his new job, his father's bottle top collection

b Tom liked: (any of these answers) how he could go to the creek and catch yabbies, walk down to the shops and know everybody, play cricket in the backyard with his Dad

4 a False; b True; c True; d True

5 Because her parents are archeologists and so are interested in ancient civilisations—and Cleopatra is a famous queen of ancient Egypt.

How was it written?

1 Paragraph 1: the name of the book, its author and theme; Paragraph 2: the story setting and the main character; Paragraph 3: some of the most important events of the plot; Paragraph 4: how the story develops; Paragraph 5: the reviewer's overall opinion

2 Tom and Cleo

3 Because that would spoil it for the audience who might want to get the book and read it.

4 IMPORTANT

5 RECOMMENDATION: I particularly recommend it for children between the ages of 11 and 14 (and their parents!).

Spelling and meaning

1 a recommend; b obsession; c humour; d particularly; e attempts; f author; g novel; h verse; i theme; j desperately; k yearns; l forgiveness; m wicked; n friendship; o characters

2 a AMUSING; b HUMOROUS; c HILARIOUS; d WITTY; e COMICAL

3 a PLOT; b CHARACTERS; c THEME; d DIALOGUE; e ACTION; f ATMOSPHERE; g SETTING; h ILLUSTRATIONS; i LAYOUT; j LANGUAGE; k WRITING STYLE

4 a SEA ANIMALS; b ROCKS; c INSECTS; d FOSSILS

Grammar

1 a The <u>tiny</u> creature ends up saving all the children. F

b The book tells the tale of an <u>imaginary</u> tribe who lived 3000 years ago. F

c The film was <u>confusing</u> because there were so many characters. O

d The story is set in a <u>magical</u> land beyond the North Pole. F

e The story takes place in a <u>haunted</u> house. F

f The ending of the film was so <u>terrifying</u>, I could not watch. O

2 a sad; b light-hearted; c action-packed; d weird; e wacky; f believable; g unbelievable; h extraordinary; i magical; j fascinating; k tense; l monotonous

Punctuation

1 a Harry Potter's friends were Hermione and Ron.

b The book tells the story of the women's struggle for freedom.

c The teachers' staffroom is the last place Bill wants to be at lunchtime.

d The mouse's tail gets chopped off quite early in the story.

e The sword becomes the symbol of the children's quest.

f The boys' terrible argument leads to disaster.

2 a Many readers will find the story difficult to follow.

b None of Mira's classmates will speak to her.

c Jason believes the neighbours might be aliens.

d The twins' inheritance changes their lives.

e His little sister's diary reveals the horrible truth.

f Hank desperately wants to play in the men's soccer team.

Can you help?

<u>Harry Potter and the Prisoner of Azkaban</u> is the third film of the Harry Potter book series by J.K. Rowling. Like the earlier films it takes us into the magical world of Harry and his two trusted friends, Ron and Hermione.

This film finds Harry and his friends in their third year at Hogwarts. A serial killer, Sirius Black, has escaped from the wizard prison, Azkaban. Sirius was the friend of Harry's parents who gave them up to Lord Voldemort. Everyone believes that Sirius is now after Harry.

I enjoyed this film more than the two earlier ones because it was much scarier. I also liked the new characters such as Sirius Black and Professor Lupin. However, there were parts of the book left out that I thought were important to include—for example, the connection between Harry's father, Sirius and Professor Lupin. The special effects were as brilliant as ever. If you are a Harry Potter fan, you must not miss Harry Potter and the Prisoner of Azkaban.

Puzzle time

a THE UGLY DUCKLING
b STAR WARS
c WIND IN THE WILLOWS
d HOME ALONE
e REVOLTING RHYMES
f THE MUDDLE-HEADED WOMBAT
g FANTASTIC MR FOX
h POSSUM MAGIC
i SNOW WHITE AND THE SEVEN DWARVES

Chapter 9 Pages 66–73

What did you read?

1 Methods of communication that do not involve words
2 a False; b True; c True; d False; e True
3 a paragraph 2; b paragraph 1; c paragraph 4; d paragraph 3
4 Because it is quicker and easier to use. (Auslan is made up from the words Australian Sign Language.)
5 Because it is too noisy to communicate by speaking. Also communication is needed over great distances, and in the past people did not have telephones or other modern technology to communicate over distance.

Note: here are the meanings of the smiley symbols (also called 'emoticons'): smiling, happy; winking, only joking; surprised (wow); unhappy; crying; angry; hugs and kisses.

How was it written?

1 c 2 12 3 HEADINGS, PARAGRAPHS
4 TOPIC. **Paragraph 2:** Many indigenous cultures, such as the Aboriginal Australians and American Indians, used ancient sign language systems to communicate silently or across great distances. **Paragraph 3:** All cultures, however, use face, hand and body gestures to show others how we think and feel. **Paragraph 4:** One special kind of sign language is the finger alphabet used by people who cannot hear. **Paragraph 5:** Communicating with flags, smoke, fire and drums are other kinds of sign systems.
5 These sentences are about the personal experiences of the author and are not suitable for a factual report.

Spelling and meaning

1 a sign
b exactly, alphabet
c imitating, indigenous
d communication
e two (language, methods, certain, cultures, ancient, systems, gestures, announce, symbols)

2 a INJURE; b PICTURE; c MEASURE; d PRESSURE; e TREASURE; f LEISURE; g MOISTURE

3 a sign(s)/symbols; methods/systems; language/communication
b i. certain; ii. exactly; iii. indigenous; iv. imitating; v. cultures; vi. alphabet; vii. ancient; viii. gestures

Grammar

a ii. Cryptologists are people whose job is breaking secret codes.
b v The science of breaking codes is cryptology, which means "secret word" in Greek.
c iv. Ciphers are codes that are made by scrambling letters.
d iii. Street signs and street lights are codes that everyone knows about.
e vii. A secret code is a code that only a few people know.
f i. Braille is a kind of code that was developed to help the blind read.
g vi. Computers use a code that translates everything into "on" or "off" terms.
h viii. No one knew the secret place where he had hidden the key.

Punctuation

2 **a** A system of black and white smoke is used in St Peter's Square in Rome to show if a new Pope has been selected in the Vatican.
b The International Code of Signals is a system of coloured flags standing for numbers and letters.
c The Morse Code system of dots and dashes was very important for communication in World War One.
d A young blind man called Louis Braille invented a brilliantly simple system to enable blind people to read with their fingers. It is called Braille after its inventor.

Can you help?

The Morse Code was invented by Samuel Morse in 1837. Morse had just invented a machine that could send electrical impulses over wires across great distances. It was called the "electric telegraph". However, the machine could not send words, so Morse had to invent a system of communication to make it useful. Morse decided to base his system on short and long clicks. The short clicks would be shown as dots in his code and the long clicks would be shown as dashes. Morse worked out which letters were used most in the English language and gave them the simplest click combinations. Morse Code can be used anywhere, as long as you have something that makes a sound. You can also send Morse Code using torches—short flashes for dots and long flashes for dashes.

Puzzle time

1 E, T and A. Here is the full list of letters from most to least frequently used: ETAONRISHDLFMCUGYPWBVKXJQZ
2 SOS, Over and out, Danger
3 MORSE TOAD
4 Lie down. Look around. Go back. He's behind you.

Chapter 10 — Pages 74–81

What did you read?

1 True
2 You should have ticked a, c, d, e.
3 b
4 Global warming and the hole in the ozone layer
5 Humans would see they were all part of the one species.

How was it written?

1 TOPIC, CLEAR
2 a
3 To help the reader follow his arguments (or a similar answer).
4 The film *E.T: The Extra-terrestrial* shows how things could go wrong (paragraph 2); For example, if Earth becomes impossible to live on because of global warming, the hole in the ozone layer … (paragraph 3)
5 To sum up
6 a

Spelling and meaning

1 **a** extraterrestrial; **b** impossible, universe; **c** quest, search; **d** definitely; **e** question; **f** arguments; **g** alien; **h** intelligence, knowledge
2 **a** **super:** over, greater or better than; **sub:** beneath, under; **trans:** across; **inter:** between
b i. transmission; ii. submerge; iii. subterranean; iv. supernova; v. interchange; vi. intergalactic

Grammar

1 **a** We will certainly need to find another planet to live on. 1; We might need to find another planet to live on. 3; We will need to find another planet to live on. 2
b We should use the money for problems here on Earth. 2; We must use the money for problems here on Earth. 1; We could use the money for problems here on Earth. 3
c Finding aliens could teach us something about ourselves. 2; Finding aliens is sure to teach us something about ourselves. 1; Finding aliens might possibly teach us something about ourselves. 3
d We should definitely put money towards more space exploration. 1; Perhaps we

should put money towards more space exploration. 3; We should probably put money towards more space exploration. 2

Punctuation

1 a Unidentified Flying Object—UFO;
  b International Space Station—ISS;
  c Extrasensory Perception—ESP;
  d National Aeronautic and Space Administration—NASA

2 a UFO; b NASA; c ISS; d ESP

Can you help?

I feel that spending large amounts of money for SETI is a complete waste of money. First of all, there are many problems on our own planet. For example, there are millions of people in developing countries who are starving. As well as this (OR also) there are children in our own cities who are homeless and on drugs. Also (OR As well as this), there are farmers who are always struggling because of drought. Secondly, we won't find any life on other planets. I think we would have heard from someone already if they were out there.

Puzzle time

1 Some words are: exit, extra, last, late, lest, rail, rare, rat, rate, real, rear, rest, retreat, retrial, sail, sale, sat, sear, seat, sire, stair, star, stare, start, tail, tale, tar, tart, taste, tear, test, tire, trail, treat, trial. Did you get any others?

2 1. ALIEN; 2. SIGNALS; 3. TAKE-OFF; 4. ROCKET; 5. ORBIT; 6. NEPTUNE; 7. AIR; 8. UFO; 9. TERRESTRIAL; ASTRONAUT

Chapter 11 Pages 82–89

Finding information

1 a You might have ticked: A Greek house; Markets, money and trade; Daily life in the city; The role of women; Childhood and education; Culture; Sport, athletics and the Olympic Games; Temples, worship and beliefs

  b The chapter "Daily life in the city" is likely to have most information.

2 Possible words are: daily life, ordinary life, life in cities, life in countries.

Using your own words

Possible answer:

A typical day for a Greek man or woman began with a trip to the "agora" or market place. A woman—either the mistress of the house or a servant of the household—might first walk around the shops in the "stoa", which was a U- or L-shaped building protected from the sun. Then she might look at the fruit and vegetables, cheese, eggs and meat brought in fresh from the countryside by the farmers. She might also look in the workshops where the craftsmen sold their wares. A man might spend most time looking for work, changing or borrowing money, or looking for slaves. Or he might just relax and chat with friends in the shade of the stoa colonnades.

Writing a bibliography

Brooks, J. 1999, *Athens*, Tuttle Publishers, London

Martins University, *Greek Mythology* (website) www.myths.martins.edu.au

Nolan, A., 2000, *Life in Ancient Greece*, Jansens, New York

Tagg, K., "Greek Treasures", *Northern News*, 3/2/04